CALL ⸢
A

MW01003173

Walter Chantry

Walter Chantry is an author who has consistently put his finger on the particular weaknesses and failures of the contemporary church. In his books we hear echoes of the prophetic insights and warnings which run through Scripture. *Call the Sabbath a Delight* is no exception. Its title indicates the burden of its message. A startling transformation has taken place in the way Christians approach the Lord's Day. While Walter Chantry does not flinch from stressing that the effects of this have been disastrous – morally and socially, as well as spiritually – his burden is not morally negative. His concern is to show why and how the Lord's Day is meant to be one of joy and blessing for God's people. He succeeds in a remarkable way. *Call the Sabbath a Delight* is written with a deep pastoral concern. It is an important book for all Christians to read.

Walter J. Chantry has been Pastor of Grace Baptist Church, Carlisle, Pennsylvania, U.S.A. since 1963. He is the author of Today's Gospel – Authentic or Synthetic, Signs of the Apostles, God's Righteous Kingdom, The Shadow of the Cross *and* Praises for the King of Kings, *also published by the Trust.*

CALL THE SABBATH A DELIGHT

WALTER J. CHANTRY

THE BANNER OF TRUTH TRUST

THE BANNER OF TRUTH TRUST
3 Murrayfield Road, Edinburgh EH 12 6EL
PO Box 621, Carlisle, Pennsylvania 17013, USA

*

© *Walter J. Chantry 1991*
First published 1991
ISBN 0 85151 588 6

*

Typeset at The Spartan Press Ltd,
Lymington, Hants
Printed and bound in Great Britain
BPCC Hazell Books
Aylesbury, Bucks, England
Member of BPCC Ltd.

Contents

Introduction   7

1. The Commandment is Holy   15

2. The Commandment is Spiritual   30

3. The Commandment is Good   43

4. Does the New Testament Teach the Fourth   52
   Commandment?

5. Sabbath Observance: Mosaic and Christian   61

6. Motives for Sabbath-Keeping   71

7. Which Day of the Week is the Sabbath?   82

8. Difficult Cases of Conscience   97

List of Outstanding Materials on the Sabbath   110

Introduction

Save yourselves from this corrupt generation.
[Acts 2:40]
Do not conform any longer to the pattern of this world.
[Romans 12:2]

. . . that you may become blameless and pure, children of God without fault in a crooked and depraved generation.
[Philippians 2:15]

When a Christian's mind turns to analysis of his social environment there comes inward discomfort and, at times, acute pain. Sorrow fills our hearts as we ponder the moral climate of the age in which we live. Our generation is corrupt, crooked and depraved. So great is the magnitude of evil in our human world that we cannot mentally or emotionally fathom it all at once. Even a small portion of the wickedness of our times can be shocking when it is seen near at hand. Thus our examination of modern ills must proceed by looking at our culture through the lenses of the Ten Commandments, taking them only one at a time. Solutions to the vice and misery of our society must also be managed as we seek to apply God's moral laws, one by one.

Have you ever been in a thoughtful mood, meditating on the crookedness of our generation, as you ushered your children into the family car on a Lord's Day morning? As you are on your way to Sunday

School and public worship, you will have noticed that the highways are already filling with cars and trucks. However, you know that most of these do not have a church for their destination. A majority of the vehicles will find their way to hunting, fishing, or hiking sites, golf courses, amusement parks, sporting contests, fairs, concerts and beaches. Our Sunday Schools are not very full.

You may pass a large public school en route to your church building. Public education is in moral crisis. Drug and alcohol addiction is for our youth a serious threat which brings enormous suffering and ruin to individuals, families and society at large. Promiscuous sexual practices are uncontrolled among large numbers of our teens. Although attempts are made to keep such matters quiet, both rebellion against authority and suicide are on the rise. Educators are concerned and promise to teach 'values'. Yet the Christian knows that our schools are determined never to teach the fear of God, which is the foundation of moral strength. If only the young people would attend churches where true morality is taught! If only one day each week were devoted to leading them to fear God and to understand his commandments!

Many families will not take their troubled and misled teens to any church. Those who wish to do so are hindered by the very schools which claim that they want parental help in training our youth. If a young man or young woman wishes to participate in whole-some school activities (play in a band, sing in a choir, join an athletic team, or even enter a project in the science fair) commitment must be made to Sunday participation. Children whose families are strongly knit to churches are forced into difficult decisions of either refusing to enter school programmes or pulling back from their churches. Schools are helping to undermine the very moral influences they claim desperately to desire. As you drive you think of the crookedness of our social order. How can it be made straight?

Upon arrival at your church building your eyes search among those assembling for worship. Where is the waitress you invited to church (or the service station attendant you asked along to Sunday School)? Your suspicions are confirmed. Of course they cannot attend worship! Sunday is the busiest day of all for restaurants and service stations. You know that on your way home you will see church-goers lined up at the gas pumps and flocking to the restaurants. How foolish to imagine that those you invited could attend public worship!

You glance at a man or woman recently divorced. At least this person is in the assembly of saints today. However, your mind surveys the painful tragedy of this case. Both husband and wife were professing Christians! Divorce is now very much a reality within the evangelical and Reformed churches. This couple had two careers to juggle. They drifted apart. They hurried together for an hour each Sunday morning, but then they were off to separate activities. They had no close common friends, even in the church. They were on the fringes. They never really shared together in any mutually undertaken service to the Lord. If only they had made it a pattern to fellowship with the saints together, serve the Lord together, study and pray together one day each week!

Your thought is interrupted as you stop to speak to a college student, a fine young person who attends a local college. He does come to church on Sunday mornings, but his understanding of the faith and of practical godliness is just not increasing. Of course he is one of the very few out of the thousands at this college who even bother to get out of bed on Sunday morning. His is a lonely trek to your church and back. Then, after one hour spent with God's people he is plunged back into the humanistic and godless atmosphere of the academic world for the rest of Sunday. The Lord's Day afternoon will be spent studying at the library, playing tennis, or in the dormitory room writing a term paper or 'horsing around'. Wouldn't someone like him, with a quick mind, grow rapidly if he gave a day each week to Christian study, worship, fellowship and service?

When Sunday School begins, it is announced that there is to be a special event for the children and adults today. With beaming satisfaction the Sunday School superintendent announces that all will stay together today to hear the testimony of a professional athlete. Everyone recognizes the name. There is rapt attention, such as God's Word seldom receives, even in the church. The assembly is pleased to know that this outstanding celebrity is a 'committed Christian'.

You are not impressed with this Christian's 'commitment'. He excuses himself from all public worship of God 26 weeks per year. He and his team mates lead tens of thousands to glue themselves to the TV set on Sunday or to spend the entire day at the stadium. Previously, you have expressed your doubts that such influences should be set before our youth as models of Christian behaviour. Who has done more to destroy patterns of worship than the professional athletes? You dare not say it again. Evangelicals themselves will fall all over one another to watch the Christian star's performances, even on Sundays.

You can recall how brothers in the Lord argued that the Sabbath law was not intended for the Christian era; it was meant only for the Jews. These noble theological positions justify one's spending a meagre hour in church followed by an eager rush to join the world in all its pursuits of business and pleasure. We do not wonder that attendance at Sunday evening services is diminishing rapidly. Some good evangelicals, who attend large churches with multiple services, can get their worship out of the way by 9:30 a.m. and be off sooner to the main business of the day. Roman Catholics have begun to go to Mass Saturday night. This is not because they believe that one should worship on the seventh day. They just want nothing to interfere with Sunday's entire day at the beach or on the golf course.

As you drive home, it is as you expected. Shopping malls are doing brisk business. Restaurants are jammed with Christian and non-Christian alike. Now the roadways are quite full. It is the great day of hedonism in our Western world. A few cars carrying believers home from church are lost in a sea of frantic pursuit of pleasure and wealth.

Is it practicable to worship God for one whole day in each seven? Can you be right about the fourth commandment and even your evangelical friends be mistaken? Such a thought quickly passes. There can be no other answer to straighten out our crooked generation. Nothing but a weekly day of worship will begin to touch the ignorance which has gripped humanity. This alone, under God, can save families, churches, schools and governments from total moral collapse.

In their pride, men have dismissed God's perfect law. His Decalogue requires the habit, the steady routine practice, the discipline of a day of worship and service to

God. It is such habit, routine and discipline that will give men both a knowledge of God and moral standards by which to live. It is just such a Sabbath Day that will strengthen families and social institutions. No wonder the church herself is devotionally, doctrinally and morally weak. Even Christians will not devote a day each week to their Lord.

Ours has become an antinomian society. It is impatient of laws, of rules and regulations. People respond angrily to demands for discipline or sacrifice. Instantaneous solutions are demanded for all social ills. Charismatics are popular just because they offer immediate miraculous answers to all of our woes through one emotional experience. That is much more attractive to modern man than a day of worship, study, prayer and service week after week.

Perhaps reformed churches have dreamed of their own quick fix through 'revival'. It is imagined by some that revival will instantaneously resolve our social torments. But, if true revival does come, it will restore righteousness to God's people. Restoration will not come in an hour's meeting, though it may begin there. Only as God's people return to the habit of engaging in systematic spiritual exercises for an entire day each week, then will the moral fabric of our age begin to be strengthened.

Whether or not people keep the Sabbath holy is not an incidental or insignificant matter. When God issued this fourth commandment he understood humanity much better than we do. Failure to practise this moral law is a root cause of moral decline, social disorder and widespread human suffering. No successful recovery of mankind can be devised without the inclusion of the fourth commandment in the remedy.

It is, then, urgent that Christians be clear in their thinking about Sabbath observance. We should consider it nothing less than shockingly unacceptable for Bible teachers and ministers to undermine the practice of the worship and service of God by teaching against the Sabbath law.

So weakened have Christians become that most of them are not accustomed to thinking about moral laws. Biblical teaching regarding the function of God's law in the life of the Christian and in society is either chaotic or non-existent in many churches. Our generation has a deep need to be instructed in Sabbath keeping. However, this essential issue of morality is being kept even from church-attenders by a host of forces. Some ministers are ignorantly fearful of mentioning any law. Some church leaders have never even studied the issue of the law and the gospel. These remain silent. Antinomians angrily rant against the fourth commandment. Legalists make the law unpalatable and twist it dangerously.

If so many devices are producing a smokescreen of confusion which obscures the Sabbath from view, you may be certain that an important truth is to be found behind the haze. All of the devices of the wicked one are employed to muddle Christian thinking only when the issue in question is of great importance to the spiritual welfare of mankind. It will be well worth your while to study through the issue of the Sabbath Day. This is a critical moral topic for our gravely corrupt generation.

THE COMMANDMENT IS HOLY

Remember the Sabbath day by keeping it holy. Six days you shall labour and do all your work, but the seventh day is a Sabbath to the LORD your God. On it you shall not do any work, neither you, nor your son or daughter, nor your manservant or maidservant, nor your animals, nor the alien within your gates. For in six days the LORD made the heavens and the earth, the sea, and all that is in them, but he rested on the seventh day. Therefore the LORD blessed the Sabbath day and made it holy.

[Exodus 20:8–11]

We live in an exceedingly busy society. Pressures of too much to do bring about tragic results. One of the great sources of sadness and suffering in children and youth is their having parents so absorbed in other things that they have no time for their sons and daughters. There is no time to read to them, no time to play with them, no time to become acquainted with what are the concerns of their children's hearts. The very young can scarcely express the ache of experiencing the fact that mummy and daddy have no time for them.

Wives, too, complain that husbands have no time for them. They are too occupied elsewhere to talk with their brides about what really matters to them both. There is no time to share activities they both used to enjoy, no time to work together on mutual goals.

Is there any greater insult than to say to another person, 'I don't have any time for you!'? Of course, it is usually not said in words but in persistent neglect and by cutting others out of one's life. This may be done by filling time with other things until no time remains for a friend. Is there any greater compliment than to say, 'I always have time for *you*'? You can offer no higher favour than to give another your undivided attention, thus demonstrating that he or she is important to you. With time we say: 'I want to know what you think. I want to show that I love you. I want to be with you and share with you. These things are vital to me.'

If human relationships are tragically broken and people are deeply wounded by our not having time for them, what of your relationship with God? Surely you have time for the One who made you! If you are a Christian, you know that the Lord made you for himself. He made you in his image to fellowship with you, to tell you what is on his mind and heart. He created you in his likeness to walk with him and talk with him and please him.

You do have time for the God who chose you from eternity to be his special people, don't you? He washed away your sins by the death of his Son so that you could be his precious ones, his very own. The Lord Jesus went to the cross, that where he is there you would also be. He has gone into the heavens to prepare for you a place at his side and his Father's side. No doubt you do have abundant time to commune with the Father and the Son. You would not insult the Most High by being too busy for him!

Time for the Lord is the issue about which the fourth commandment speaks. Both Old and New Testaments inform us that the moral rule of highest significance is to love the Lord our God with all of our hearts. The principal ingredient of human morality is loving the

Almighty. Anyone who fails to love the Lord Jehovah is guilty of the gravest crime.

How is love to be expressed? What is the behaviour of love? Paul has taught us that 'love is the fulfillment of the law', (*Romans 13:10*). God's moral law defines what loving activity is. The Ten Commandments, written by the finger of God on tables of stone at Mount Sinai, are the Lord's summary of moral law, his definition of loving behaviour.

Most prominent in the Ten Commandments is love to God. Four commandments outlining expected love for our Maker are the first and the most lengthy portion of this code of conduct. Such prominence signifies that love to God is the critical issue in human ethics. The first commandment shows that love to our God requires our exclusive worship of him and service to him. The second prescribes the manner in which love will worship and serve the Lord. The third specifies the attitude of reverence which love will bring to God's worship and service. The fourth stipulates what time is required to express our love to him. So long as we are creatures of time, love must devote time unto him who is the object of our supreme love. When time shall be no more, we shall be forevermore in his immediate presence.

Our Creator's moral commandments are very modest in their requests of his creatures. He is most reasonable and generous toward you. Only one day in seven is to be devoted entirely to his worship and service. Six full days are granted to you to pursue all your legitimate interests of work and recreation. 'Six days you shall labour and do all *your* work, but the seventh day is a Sabbath *to the* LORD *your God*.'

God gave us the entire planet earth to use for our

welfare and to enjoy to the full. He asked only that a tenth (or tithe) be returned to him in recognition of his being Lord over all. Wouldn't you love to see your taxes fall to ten per cent? But the Lord who sends you sun and rain and has freely given you all resources of land and animals and minerals and life and talent from which you make your profits required only a tenth. So too the One who has given you all the years of your earthly life and the hope of eternal life beyond this one asks in return one day in seven to be devoted to him.

Some complain that an entire day each week is too much to ask. Men simply do not have that much time for God. Sadly, we must say that a vast part of humanity does not so much as think about this moral obligation. Because it is the most quickly forgotten moral law, Jehovah begins, 'Remember the Sabbath day.' Men are apt to be unaware of this aspect of love to God. It is one of the first issues having to do with Biblical principles of conduct to which the human conscience is deadened. In our day even the vast majority of evangelical Christians act as if they have never heard of this moral issue regarding the time that God asks of us. A college student once wrote a tract with the satirical title, 'I Believe in All Nine of the Ten Commandments'. He wished to shock Christians out of their habit of ignoring the fourth commandment.

God's moral requirement that we express our love to him by devoting a portion of time to his worship and service is not difficult to understand. It is neither complex nor marked by a multiplicity of rules and regulations. There are four very simple principles given us in the fourth commandment which no loving heart will find puzzling or burdensome. Two of the general principles are positive and two are negative.

First we are to 'remember the Sabbath day'. It is to be kept in mind as an important obligation and commitment. We may sincerely intend to devote the whole of a child's birthday to being with him. However, should we forget the day, we may make it impossible to keep our promise. Business appointments are made on that day. Recreation plans with friends are scheduled. Soon the hours of the birthday are filled with other things. Pressures upon our time require of us the discipline of ensuring that we are free from other arrangements if we are going to devote a portion of time to a loved one. Care must be taken to finish our work so that demands upon us do not spill over into the day given to another. It is just the same with the Lord's Day.

Love which desires to commune with God and to serve God will not forget the time scheduled to be given to our Lord. Effort will be made to keep the assigned hours. The Sabbath Day must be taken into consideration in our scheduling of work and play. Time for the Lord will be blocked out and guarded so far as we are humanly able to do so. The day must be remembered and taken into account. Our time must be managed so that the day is available to the Lord.

A second positive general principle is that the day is to be kept holy. 'Remember the Sabbath day by keeping it holy.' So insensitive have men become to God's moral law that we must point out that the fourth commandment is speaking of an entire day. Reference is not merely made to a few hours for church attendance. One entire day in each cycle of seven days is to be kept holy. Six days may be spent in our own work but the seventh is the Sabbath of the Lord our God.

An entire day is to be 'kept holy'. By this the Scripture means that it is to be set aside from ordinary use to be devoted to the Lord God. This portion of time is for sacred use – to worship and serve the Lord. When tables and bowls and forks were called 'holy' in Old Testament times, it was meant that they were no longer to be employed in common ways. They were to be devoted exclusively to sacred usage. They were set aside for activities related to the worship and service of God. In similar fashion, this commandment requires that a day of time be completely dedicated to spiritual uses. 'The seventh day (as opposed to six used for our own business) is a Sabbath to the LORD your God.' It is his day. He has staked out a claim upon it. It belongs to him.

This is not a narrow or restrictive requirement. A heart that loves the Lord will leap for joy at the prospect of a day with him. Doesn't a child love to have a day with his father? Of course the worldly will loathe giving any time to God. The self-absorbed will regret any day spent in his presence. Without love for God such a requirement will seem narrow and a heavy burden. But for the godly it is a broad road of liberty and joy. There is an entire day each week liberated from my ordinary recreations and labours to serve the lover of my soul and to be with him.

If a Christian takes a bit of time on the Sabbath for private Bible reading and prayer, if he is faithful in public worship on God's holy day, if time is spent teaching his children God's Word, time preparing and teaching a Bible lesson, time visiting the sick and poor in Jesus' name, time witnessing to a friend, time fellowshipping with the saints, time singing praises to God – soon the day seems all too short for the spiritually minded. There is so much to do for God in private, in the family, in the church. There is so much to do in worship and praise. It is a holy day, different from the other six. It is devoted to the Lord in his worship and service.

Along with the two positive principles to remember the day and to keep it holy, there are two negative requirements. The two negatives really clarify what it is to keep the day holy. One cannot do the two forbidden things and still sanctify the day. Keeping the day holy is exclusive of two things forbidden.

'On it you shall not do any work.' Normal labours must not intrude into the time of the Sabbath Day. The time is to be devoted to the Lord. If personal business or family business or studies for school or work for an employer or community affairs take our time, the time is taken away from that which ought to be devoted to the Lord. The fourth commandment is not merely to remember Sunday School and church hours to keep them holy. If it were, we could watch baseball and football all afternoon and evening, or we could go back to our ordinary employments. This must not be. On the 'day' we are not to do any work.

The day of worship is called the 'Sabbath' which means rest or cessation from labour. However, inactivity or non-exertion is not the issue intended. We are not to imagine that he keeps the Sabbath most holy who sleeps the most or remains motionless. The point of resting from our own work is to free up the time to worship and serve God energetically. In a later chapter we will note our Saviour's comments on this very misconception encouraged by the Pharisees.

Much has been written regarding the benefits of a day spent resting. Indeed there is a hint of this in

Scripture when we are told that our animals are not to work on this day. They have no souls with which to commune with God, but they too are to rest. When Jonah preached of the coming wrath of God upon Nineveh, not only did the people of that great city fast in humiliation before the Lord; food was also withheld from the cattle, who could not share in the spiritual exercises of which fasting was a part. They could however participate in the physical aspects. Perhaps there are great psychological and physical benefits to be received from not spending all our days in similar activity. A change of pace will bring us material benefits. Nevertheless the intent of the day is not rest, absolutely considered. It is rest from our works so that we may give ourselves to the Lord on that day. His worship and his service may be quite as demanding as our own employments.

A second negative general principle is that we are not to employ others to work for us on God's holy day, not sons, daughters, servants, animals, or aliens. If we are obligated to love the Lord our God, others are under equal obligation. If loving God requires that we spend one day in each seven worshipping and serving our Maker and Redeemer, the rest of mankind is under the same debt. They too must keep the time on this day exclusively for the Lord. We must not divert them from the worship and service of the Lord or tempt them to desecrate the day which is holy.

In a heathen culture one is tempted to reason that the 'stranger' to God's covenants or the 'alien' to the household of God will work anyway. He will not make it a matter of conscience to devote a day to his Maker. His shop will be open. Why not let his hours of employment serve me and make the Lord's Day more pleasant for me? God's commandment forbids this process of thought by forbidding us even to employ the alien in work for us on God's holy day. God's moral laws are of universal application. They are not intended only for believers.

Every rule of ethics may be made to sound complicated by bringing to it a host of questions about its application. It is a favourite tactic of those who oppose any moral law to propose extremely difficult circumstances in which application of our code of conduct seems unmanageable, or in which one principle appears to be in conflict with another. In this way the standard is declared absurd and impracticable. The fourth commandment is not exempt from such treatment. It is important that, before you face the dazzling complexities of supposed difficult cases, you ponder the simplicity and practicality of this law.

One day in each seven is to be kept in mind and set aside, its time being devoted to sacred things – the worship and service of the true and living God. Normal business and recreation are not to take up our hours on this day, nor are we to employ others to labour for us. A child may easily understand the requirement. That is not to say that the law is easily kept. 'Do not covet' is not difficult to understand, but we experience agonies in wrestling with our flesh to comply with God's law! And what complexities arise in seeking to apply this God-given rule in daily living.

After the fourth commandment explains the Sabbath requirement, three reasons or incentives are given within the law itself to strengthen our resolve to obey it. As every student of the Bible knows, the Ten Commandments are very ancient. They were first delivered to the human race in written form by Moses at Mount Sinai. (Long before that they had been written on the human conscience. This was done at the time of Adam's creation – Romans 2:15. Through regeneration God's Spirit indelibly imprints them upon the desires of the heart – Hebrews 10:15, 16. Thus do believers run in the way of God's commandments.) God's written fourth commandment recalls the first historic observance of the Sabbath in order to stir up our own compliance with Sabbath-keeping.

The particular historic incident God cites for us goes back to the creation of the world. 'For in six days the LORD made the heavens and the earth, the sea, and all that is in them, but he rested on the seventh day.' In the week of time during which all our world and its creatures were created, the Triune God himself worked all his creative activity for six days but rested on the seventh. Therefore, man is to imitate his Creator by working only six of each seven days and by resting on one.

Our Lord's argumentation is extremely important for a number of reasons. First it will be noted that this is not a peculiarly Jewish ordinance. The reason which the Almighty gave for keeping the Sabbath was not rooted in anything unique to Jewish experience. Its foundation is laid upon creative reality. Because of the divine pattern of activity and rest in his creation work, we too are to follow a similar cycle of labour and rest. As we have already noted, strangers to the covenants of Israel and aliens from the household of God's people are also under an obligation to observe this moral law, for they are creatures whose very beings are owed to divine creative labour.

Some have attempted to exempt believers in the Christian era from any responsibility to keep the fourth commandment. They do so with elaborate arguments designed to show that this law is unique to Judaism and has been suspended with the coming of Christ. It is true that, just before entering Canaan, when Moses rehearsed the Ten Commandments to Israel (*Deuteronomy 5*), he did urge upon the Hebrews deliverance from Egypt as a reason to keep the Sabbath. But as originally given on Mount Sinai (*Exodus 20*), the fourth law was enforced with an argument from God's behaviour during creation week.

Jewish peculiarities did indeed attach themselves to the fourth commandment as to every one of the ten. Ceremonial and judicial regulations unique to Judaism do engulf the keeping of the Sabbath in Old Testament times just as they do the honouring of parents. It is true that care must be taken in the study of most Old Testament passages to separate moral law from ceremonial and judicial additions. We are not required in New Testament times to apply the fourth commandment as the Hebrews did, using their ceremonies and their civil enforcements. But the Ten Commandments *per se* are free of all ceremonial and judicial peculiarities of the Mosaic covenant.

Exodus 20:11 takes us back beyond Moses and Abraham. The very words used in the latter part of the verse are recorded in Genesis 2:1–3:

Thus the heavens and the earth were completed in all their vast array. By the seventh day God had finished the work he had been doing; so on the seventh day he rested from all his work. And God blessed the seventh day and made it holy, because on it he rested from all the work of creating that he had done.

The two additional reasons we must consider as

incentives to keep the Sabbath are that God blessed the Sabbath Day and that he himself made it holy. This text tells us when God set apart the day for himself and for sacred use by others. It was not after the Jews left Egypt. His declaration that the day belonged to him was issued in creation week, at the time he personally observed the first rest.

At the time of creation the Almighty published his claim that one day in seven had been devoted to him and at that same time he proclaimed blessing upon the day. It appears that Cain and Abel were aware of this seven day cycle, six for work and one for rest to worship the Lord. Genesis 4:3 tells us that the two brothers brought their sacrifices to God 'in the course of time' or, literally, 'at the end of days', that is on the seventh day. Adam's sons knew that there was a day of worship each week. Noah gave great attention to the seven day cycle of time. In Exodus 16, before the Ten Commandments were given, manna was given to the Jews. They were reminded without explanation that the seventh day is 'a day of rest, a holy Sabbath to the Lord' (*verse 23*). It was presumed that they would understand this ancient creation law.

Still others have dismissed the fourth commandment by suggesting that it is entirely forward-looking. They would tell us that the Sabbath is a ceremony prefiguring rest in Christ or rest from salvation by works by trusting in grace. Again, through elaborate theological reasoning, they would lead us to think that the Sabbath, like sacrifices and the temple, is a shadow of Christ and his gospel. The Sabbath or the shadow may now be discarded because the reality is here. But the commandment does not explicitly point to Christ or to future fulfillment. It explicitly looks *back* to past creative work and rest by God. A Sabbath is to be kept by men in imitation of God's example at creation. Our life is to take on the imprint of God's image with regard to the use of time.

A second inducement for us to keep the Sabbath holy, found within the command itself, is 'Therefore the Lord blessed the Sabbath day'. Already we have noted that the 'therefore' points back to his own practice in creation week. Since the first week of time was spent by the King of Glory working six days and making the seventh day one of holy honour for himself, he pronounced a benediction upon the day of sacred worship.

There is blessing to be had in connection with keeping the Sabbath Day. Surely the reference is to blessing which falls on his creatures who enter into God's rest with him. There is great benefit and happiness heaped upon those who keep the day holy. Our heavenly Father has pledged blessing within Sabbath observance.

Where a weekly day is not spent in the worship and service of God, ignorance of God and his Word increases rapidly both in and outside the church. Families disintegrate, finding inadequate time to instruct children in morality, no time to pray together as families. Individuals are 'stressed out' because their souls are neglected and they can find no fountains of spiritual refreshment. Churches are weak and neglected. Few worshippers are present and even fewer are found who will devote time to the Lord's service within her body.

What blessings are to be found in devoting an entire day to the worship and service of the Lord? His own nearness to his people. A knowledge of the day of salvation. Fellowship with the saints. Homes in which parents worship with children, instruct children, read the Bible to children, talk with children about moral issues of our day – 52 days per year, one entire year out of every seven. Churches full of people seeking to praise God and to find avenues of service to the Lord. Nations whose thought and moral fibre are lifted toward heavenly standards. The Word of God abundantly studied. Prayer multiplied. Spiritual refreshment, joy, progress in the kingdom. Psychological strength.

How trite to proclaim that a Sabbath Day is impractical and impossible. How unspiritual to call it a burden which is hard to bear. It is impossible to conceive of any measure more perfectly designed than is the Sabbath to bring everlasting blessings to individuals, families, churches and communities. Spiritual men bemoan the lack of time to pray, read, worship, witness, teach children. God in his wisdom and grace has provided just such time for these very wishes of the godly by commanding that a day in each seven be set aside, devoted to the Lord.

Finally a third reason is given to strengthen our resolve to keep the Sabbath holy. It is that 'the Lord made it holy'. He who is King over all the earth has, by his sovereign right, made the day holy. He devoted one day in each seven to his worship and service. He does not advise or request but he decrees that it is so. He who is eternal divided our time and legislated that we give him a day of worship each week.

Since he is the lawgiver and judge it is his prerogative to institute the moral law. It is advisable that every creature take note of this reminder that the Almighty has personally set aside one day in seven for himself. All who must one day stand before him to have their everlasting destinies announced have need to hear the standard he devised to judge them. How many excuses of ignorance, of being too busy to pray, of not having time to read Scripture, to become acquainted with the saints, to bring one's family to worship will die on the lips of the guilty before this commandment? When in his awesome majesty the Lord says, 'I made the day holy', who will plead exemption from Sabbath practice?

It is the Lord who declared the day holy. Who will deny it? It is the Lord who decided that Sabbath-keeping would be one of the ten pillars of human righteousness. Who wishes to argue with him? It is the Lord who kept the first Sabbath, showing such use of time to be of the essence of divine moral character. Who will lead others to fall short of the glory of God? Who would not imitate his righteousness? or not obey his law? He has said the commandment is holy. It is an essential ingredient of righteousness.

2

THE COMMANDMENT IS SPIRITUAL

If you keep your feet from breaking the Sabbath and from doing as you please on my holy day, if you call the Sabbath a delight and the LORD's holy day honourable, and if you honour it by not going your own way and not doing as you please or speaking idle words, then you will find your joy in the LORD, and I will cause you to ride on the heights of the land and to feast on the inheritance of your father Jacob. The mouth of the LORD has spoken.

[Isaiah 58:13–14]

Have you ever determined to read through the five books of Moses? In doing so have you felt it to be burdensome to read through all of Leviticus or the latter chapters of Exodus? Perhaps you have suspected that you are unspiritual to find these lengthy lists of rules and regulations to be stark and unappealing. Imagine the poor Jew who had to live by these bleak laws! If you have felt guilty for having such thoughts creep into your mind, let Peter relieve your conscience.

At the Jerusalem council in Acts 15, 'the party of the Pharisees stood up and said, "The Gentiles must be circumcised and required to obey the law of Moses."' Such a suggestion is not only an ancient curiosity. There are modern day 'Reformed' teachers seriously proposing that all the law of Moses must be observed by Christians and by society at large, although they have not enforced circumcision as did the Pharisees. In response to this ancient (and modern) suggestion, the apostle Peter said, 'Why do you try to test God by putting on the necks of the disciples a yoke that neither we nor our fathers have been able to bear?' (*Acts 15:5–10*).

Perhaps it is not so unspiritual to view the endless detailed regulations of Moses as irksome, arduous and oppressive to the spirit. A Jewish apostle admitted that it was unbearable to live under the Jewish system. Its rules were like a yoke of slavery. It would be tempting God to place gospel disciples under such a regimen. Have the proponents of the restoration of a Mosaic-style society to our modern world listened to Peter?

Great care must be taken, however, not to place God's moral law into the same category of our thinking as is given to the ponderous judicial and ceremonial laws of Moses. For the moral law, which reflects the very righteousness of God, is not vexatious and laborious to the Christian. It is his delight. Paul, who stood with Peter and his position at the Jerusalem council, later said of the moral law: 'In my inner being I delight in God's law'; and 'we know that the law is spiritual' (*Romans 7:22 and 14*). Although Moses did add to the fourth commandment many judicial and ceremonial elements, the Sabbath requirement itself is a delightfully spiritual law.

Isaiah has often been called the evangelical prophet. That is because his book is filled with remarkably clear revelations of Jesus Christ and the gospel age. It is not difficult to preach the latter chapters of his prophecy in the New Testament times. It is not surprising then that we find in Isaiah 58 a discussion of the Sabbath in all its spiritual beauty. Here is a text in which the Sabbath law is presented without the drab and unappealing attire of judicial additives. In this place the moral law is dressed in the bright silks of its gospel finery. Isaiah emphasizes the spiritual essence of the Sabbath.

For those who keep the Sabbath as Isaiah is urging, attractive promises are held out in verse 14. Here is a divinely inspired commentary upon Exodus 20:11: 'Therefore the Lord blessed the Sabbath day.' Most spiritual blessings these promises are! And sealed with the solemn announcement, 'The mouth of the Lord has spoken.' These pleasant prospects are not to be doubted, but are underscored by divine authority. Three special blessings will undoubtedly attend keeping the Sabbath Day holy.

First to be mentioned as a blessing for Sabbath-keepers is joy in the Lord. 'Then you will find your joy in the Lord.' Some religious people have very long faces. They grumble and complain, showing that they do not have much joy in the Lord. It is possible to attend public worship, to read the Bible and pray while still being miserable and unpleasant. There is a 'sour-pickle' religion in which all is hard work, duty and trouble but no joy in the Lord. By contrast, those who understand and practise keeping the Sabbath holy will experience joy in the Lord!

Did you ever notice that you most enjoy the company of people you know really well? The companionship of close relatives and favourite friends brings deep pleasure. At times, visits with distant relatives or bare acquaintances can be tense and taxing. God is to be our familiar Father and intimate friend. Abraham was a friend of God. The Lord came to his tent and ate with him and told Abraham the secrets of his heart. In a similar way God the Son says: 'I stand at the door and knock. If anyone hears my voice and opens the door, I will come in and eat with him and he with me' (*Revelation 3:20*).

Familiarity comes only by giving time to a relationship. Even a father or a friend may become remote if there is not regular fellowship. Joy from an association fades if contact and sharing become only occasional. Each week a day is to be spent with the Lord. Such nearness to him and commitment to him produce joy in him. Our whole being is then cheered by the brightness of God's smile, the delightfulness of his praises, the rich love of his house, his people, his kingdom. Those who form the habit of keeping one day in seven holy find that the day returns to them a joy in the Lord.

Isaiah's second promise for those who keep the Sabbath is victory. 'I will cause you to ride on the heights of the land.' This ancient imagery suggests a conqueror riding in his chariot upon the heights. He is one who has achieved true success. He is victorious.

You are certainly aware of Christians who give the appearance of being beaten down. They have a 'hang-dog' look to them. They keep going, but when you talk with them you get the idea that they are losing and that they think so too. The life of faith was not intended to be like that. In his letters to the Seven Churches our Lord Jesus repeatedly holds out promises 'to him who overcomes'. Paul cried out, 'We are more than conquerors' (*Romans 8:37*). John said confidently, 'This is the victory that has overcome the world, even our faith' (*1 John 5:4*). Believers ought to have a sense of triumph over sin, death, hell, the devil, the world and the flesh.

Of course we are referring to a spiritual victory which is not of the same sort that the world gives. Daniel and his three friends were mighty conquerors even while they were alien prisoners. Christian living is not intended to be holding on by our fingernails until someone arrives in this wicked world to rescue us. We are to turn the world upside down. We are to attempt great things for God. We are to move the world around us to fear God and to think of truth and righteousness. We should ride upon the heights in triumph.

Such overcoming and conquering is not an accident. It does not mysteriously fall upon some and miss others. Success in business comes from hard work. Success in sports arises from rigid discipline and training. Still, none of these trophies will last. Real conquering in the Lord also demands time, discipline, effort. Sometimes young believers stand in awe of wise and gracious Christians. What is their secret of knowing so much of the Bible and the Lord? Why, they study Scripture and pray 52 days per year; they hear at least 52 Bible lessons and 104 sermons per year; they enjoy 52 days of public and private prayer each year. If they have walked with the Lord twenty years there have been 1,040 days, or nearly three full years of their lives, devoted largely to a study of the Scriptures and to prayer. The Sabbath Day is the Christian's training day, sharpening him for the conflict, preparing him for triumphant living in Christ.

Furthermore, Isaiah holds out the promise of feasting upon good things. 'I will cause you . . . to feast on the inheritance of your father Jacob.' A feast gives you the idea of abundance, all that your heart could wish of good things. It connotes happily eating of the most delicious fruits of one's labour to full satisfaction. A feast usually implies as well the enjoyment of sharing prosperity and celebration with others. No one feasts alone.

Again, you will not have to look far to find 'Christians' who seem to have so little. They would never say with David, 'My cup overflows.' Some who approach ministers for counsel are starving. They feel their spiritual hunger and thirst. They are so alone. Theirs is a meagre fare eaten in solitude. Normally such poorly fed 'sheep' seldom or irregularly find their way to the green pastures of Lord's Days' assemblies. The chief reason is that they have not ordered their lives to devote one day in each seven to the Lord.

It is on the Sabbath Day that the Lord's good things are served up. On this day the milk and wine may be had without money and without price. A soul may delight itself in fatness. The feast is spread, but those who will not keep the fourth commandment make excuses for not attending. No one who repeatedly excuses himself from the table may expect to feast on the riches of the house. He may pick at a bone here or there but the delicious morsels are served up in the assemblies of God's house on God's holy days. Cassette tapes, books and video recordings are poor substitutes for the Spirit-filled ministry at the family gatherings on holy feast days.

Would you like your life to be filled with joy in the Lord, triumph and feasting on the good things of God? That is what God promises to those who keep the Sabbath Day holy. The treasures of God's kingdom both now and forever will overflow to those who rightly keep the fourth commandment. Is this law designed to spoil your fun? Is a whole day spent with God something that will make you a long-faced loser who misses out on the really good times? The mouth of the Lord has declared the very opposite. With the Sabbath regulation, the Lord is taking you by the hand to lead you to joy, triumph and feasting.

It is with the enticement of charming spiritual pleasures that our Lord calls us in Isaiah 58 to keep the

Sabbath Day holy. If then you wish to savour joy, victory and feasting, give attention to Isaiah's directions. You will find them as spiritual as the promises given Sabbath-observers. An intricate list of detailed instructions is not given to us. A catalogue of 'dos and don'ts' is not provided. Instead the Lord's prophet speaks about attitude. Your frame of heart is all important to Sabbath-keeping. The outlook of your inner man is the essence of keeping the day holy.

Of the utmost importance is the attitude of cheerfulness within those who worship and serve God one day in each seven. After all has been said, 'God loves a cheerful giver' (2 *Corinthians* 9:7). That is true not only in the case of monetary gifts, but even more so with regard to the devotion of ourselves to the Almighty for an entire day each week.

Our hearts should look forward to the Sabbath as a favourite day, the most wonderful of days. You should not cast a longing eye at the world and its entertainments. It is offensive to the Lord if we approach him while preferring to be elsewhere and if we show that with pouting lip or with impatient shuffling feet that are eager to be off to other things. You must come with the sense of relish which excites the person who will meet with a lover. Even the comparison of setting aside our business and earthly pleasures should make us happy to spend a day with our favourite persons, the Father, the Son, and the Holy Spirit.

In the days of Eastern monarchs, even an earthly king would not allow subjects to enter his presence with any appearance of sadness. Such a bearing would be an insult to the king. Unhappiness would suggest that being with the ruler was an unpleasant experience. On one occasion Nehemiah was 'very much afraid'. The terror in his heart arose from the king's question, 'Why does your face look so sad?' (*Nehemiah 2:1–3*).

Unfortunately, few have thought very much about the great importance of bringing joyful worship to our God. The psalmists are an exception. For instance we read in Psalm 100: 'Shout for *joy* to the LORD, all the earth. Worship the LORD with *gladness*; come before him with *joyful* songs.' Although we must confess our sins and seek grace for further sanctification, the atmosphere of worship must not be dominated by heaviness and remorse. Ministers must learn the enormous importance of evoking joyful praise from the hearts of the people. A steady diet of conviction of sin alone will make our assemblies dreary and the Lord's Day a burden.

There must be in our hearts a positive attitude of pleasant excitement in coming to a day with the Lord. Parents must be careful of the impressions given to their children concerning the Lord's Day. Mothers and fathers must work at making the Sabbath a delight to their children. Boys and girls must not come to view days of worship as grim and repressive. Parents may convey that impression by constant 'don'ts' and scoldings. All attention must not be to external details and endless regulations. Family focus must be upon what a delight the day is.

To do this parents must remember the developmental weakness of small children. They cannot read and pray for hours without end. Their attention span may be twenty or thirty minutes. The young need bodily exercise if they are not to wiggle hopelessly in meetings. When children are denied an activity that they enjoy on other days, it should be replaced with a Sabbath activity that fills their time and delights their hearts. Parents must spend more time with children on the Lord's Day: reading Scripture stories, playing Bible memory games, going for walks where parables from creation are shown, singing psalms and hymns with them, doing catechism work together.

A house swept of the demons of the world but left empty will soon be occupied with worse demons. So too it will be with Sabbath hours. Children may be given experience in Christian service, visiting elderly and shut-ins to read a psalm and have fellowship. When parents make the Sabbath a delight to their little ones, these children forever bear pleasant memories of days given to the Lord. We are so inventive when it comes to carnal earthly delights. Why do parents throw up their hands with dismay when it comes to leading children into spiritual enjoyments?

What an interesting promise Isaiah has given! 'If you call the Sabbath a delight . . . you will find your joy in the Lord.' How can the day be a pleasure unless we rejoice in the Lord? But then how can we rejoice in the Lord if a day worshipping and serving him is a heaviness to us? The condition and the hope are bound together and mutually supportive.

If our spiritual attitude regarding Sabbath-keeping must include cheerfulness, it must also be made up of an awareness that the day is special. Our text suggests that Lord's Days must be considered extraordinary both because they are different from other days and because they are higher (more noble) than other days. With the heart this day must be treated with greater dignity, deeper appreciation, and more careful thought than the other six days. As birthdays and anniversaries receive special consideration in families, so the Lord's Day should hold a place of high esteem in the family of mankind.

An emphasis is placed on the difference between the Sabbath and other days. 'Not going your own way and not doing as you please or speaking idle words' (*verse 13*). On the other six days we may arise in the morning and think: 'What shall I plan to do today? What would I like to accomplish? What things would I like to discuss with my family and fellow workers today?' On the Sabbath we must think: 'This is the Lord's holy day. I will talk of all his greatness and his thoughts. I will do his will today.' It is when that outlook dominates your spirit on the Sabbath that you will know the joy of the Lord, triumphant living and feasting on the best things.

When such an attitude seems to anyone unreasonable and restrictive, it reveals a deep selfishness in that individual. If I were to give you seven delicious candy treats, I might tell you to keep six but that I would like you to return one to me. Only the self-centred would clutch all seven and put on a long face in response to my request. God has given you seven days. He asks that one be returned to him. Yet some think it burdensome that on one day they should not pursue wealth, go fishing, be entertained by television, or talk of sports and vacations. Such an attitude is a symptom of self-centredness. When men are in love with themselves they are unhappy in this life. Self-absorption also causes men, women, and children to perish.

Those who truly love the Lord will call his holy day 'honourable' and will honour it. It will be held in great esteem. The Sabbath is the highest of days because it belongs to the Lord in a special way. It is the day he has called his people into solemn but joyful assemblies. In these gatherings the Lord condescends to come down in special nearness to those who love him and seek him. Never must we think of the Sabbaths as bland or nothing-days. They are the most sacred of days.

Verse 13 begins with a phrase which brings us back to common modern practice. 'If you keep your feet from breaking the Sabbath . . .' Our Lord is suggesting that he has a grievance: his Sabbath is being trampled. To grind something under foot is a sign of contempt. It is not always consciously done. We only walk on that which is worthless, that which has no value, that for which we have no regard. We do not even think of the things we walk upon. Giving it no thought is the insult. Our Lord Jesus told us that salt which loses its savour 'is no longer good for anything, except to be thrown out and trampled by men'. The Lord is suggesting through Isaiah that his Sabbath has been counted as of no worth. It was being trampled under foot of men in Isaiah's day.

Signs of the same ugly attitude are legion in Western society. Sunday is filled with professional and amateur sports. It is a day of bustling markets, crowded highways, camping, hiking, partying. It has been put to every common use. But the root of all things which appear on the surface is the worst crime of all. The Sabbath is trampled by self-centred, man-centred activities because it is considered of no special worth. The lone social institution which remains uncrowded is the house of prayer. Worship of God and service to God are not specially valued. Hence the Lord's holy day has fallen into dishonour. The Sabbath is thought good for nothing, except to be thrown out and trampled by men. Trampling his special days argues a lack of love for the Lord.

Early in Isaiah 58 the prophet poses some questions being asked in his generation. Verse 3 suggests that some felt God did not see them or notice them. Why has the Lord not visited us and blessed us? Why has he abandoned us? This is a strange question from those who have so little love for God that they have no respect for his days of worship. If they would cease trampling on the Sabbath, if they would cheerfully honour the day by making it different from the other six, then God would pour out his spiritual blessings.

Isaiah has gone to the heart of the matter by going to our hearts. In the spirit of New Testament religion he has given us spiritual principles attended with spiritual promises. The prophet has shown us just how spiritual God's moral law is, emphatically how spiritual the fourth commandment is.

Isaiah's central requirement is that our inmost being call the Sabbath a delight. David expressed this poetically when he said, 'Better is one day in your courts than a thousand elsewhere' (*Psalm 84:10*). There are no other enjoyments that can compare to the bewitching pleasures of a soul transported into the presence of God. We enter the courts where he dwells by the means of grace and most especially by the public assemblies of worship. One such day of communion with God is preferred over a thousand. Surely it is relished by the godly above the other six in the week. We need not wait for a thousand ordinary days to pass us by before we approach God's courts. It is a spiritual favour to be prized that we are called by the moral law to approach his throne one

CALL THE SABBATH A DELIGHT

day in each week. When the spiritually minded reads the fourth commandment he cries, 'Direct me in the path of your commands, for there I find delight' (*Psalm 119:35*).

3

THE COMMANDMENT IS GOOD

At that time Jesus went through the grain fields on the Sabbath. His disciples were hungry and began to pick some heads of grain and eat them. When the Pharisees saw this, they said to him, 'Look! Your disciples are doing what is unlawful on the Sabbath.' He answered, 'Haven't you read what David did when he and his companions were hungry? He entered the house of God, and he and his companions ate the consecrated bread – which was not lawful for them to do, but only for the priests. Or haven't you read in the Law that on the Sabbath the priests in the temple desecrate the day and yet are innocent? I tell you that one greater than the temple is here. If you had known what these words mean, 'I desire mercy, not sacrifice,' you would not have condemned the innocent. For the Son of Man is Lord of the Sabbath.' Going on from that place, he went into their synagogue, and a man with a shrivelled hand was there. Looking for a reason to accuse Jesus, they asked him, 'Is it lawful to heal on the Sabbath?' He said to them, 'If any of you has a sheep and it falls into a pit on the Sabbath, will you not take hold of it and lift it out? How much more valuable is a man than a sheep! Therefore it is lawful to do good on the Sabbath.' Then he said to the man, 'Stretch out your hand.' So he stretched it out and it was completely restored, just as sound as the other. But the Pharisees went out and plotted how they might kill Jesus.
[Matthew 12:1–14]

We can see that Isaiah had a very positive and pleasant approach to the fourth commandment. But that is not the case with everyone! There are always people at hand who have a talent for wringing the last drop of brightness and cheer from the Sabbath. In every period of history there have been some strait-laced and acerbic spirits who managed to make the Lord's Day harrowing and bitter with endless restrictions. Self-appointed autocrats who usurp authority over other believers harass their fellow men with unrelenting strictness. Dour negativism seems often to follow on the heels of a libertine society.

It is certainly true that our modern day is lawless when it comes to the Sabbath. Few pay any attention to this part of God's law. Even churches which speak highly of the Ten Commandments pretend not to notice the fourth. Still we must be careful not to rush into the arms of an inflexible and tyrannical system which makes the Sabbath unwieldy. There do lie in wait some overbearing persons who make a legion of cumbersome external regulations out of very simple and spiritual principles. Such are to be found in modern times as in ages past.

Our Lord Jesus Christ had to contend with this temper within the Pharisees of his own days on earth. It was they who made the Sabbath dismal, crushing and intolerable in his society. Matthew, in chapter twelve of his Gospel, records two incidents in which our Lord had conflict with the Pharisees over Sabbath observance. In the two confrontations we find Jesus' mood regarding the Sabbath completely unlike that of the legalistic Pharisees. Not only is there a contrast of style, but our Saviour positively condemns the tone which the Pharisees had brought to the weekly Sabbath. His teaching will serve to indict cheerless austerity in our day as well as his.

When our Lord convinced the Pharisees of exacting too much regarding the Sabbath, we must realize that he was exposing the errors in their interpretation of the Old Testament teaching on the Sabbath. The Pharisees accused Jesus and his disciples of having broken the fourth commandment when they walked through grain fields, picked some heads of grain and ate them (*verses 1–2*). They were prepared to accuse Jesus of breaking the fourth commandment if he healed a man with a withered hand on the Sabbath (*verses 9–10*). Our Lord Jesus, in renouncing their standards, was *not* saying that the fourth commandment had become obsolete and must now be discarded.

At this time in our Lord's earthly ministry, Jesus was pledged to fulfill all righteousness even under the Mosaic judicial and ceremonial laws. It was he alone who perfectly lived by the system given under Moses. He and his disciples could not sweep away any Old Testament law as irrelevant if Jesus were to fulfill his mission as Messiah. Our Lord is not suggesting to the Pharisees that it is permissible to break the law because the law must be changed.

To the contrary, Jesus is accusing the Pharisees of a fundamental misunderstanding of the Sabbath law. Their views were entirely mistaken and could not be defended from Old Testament Scriptures. They had blundered seriously in handling Biblical passages on the law. Our Prophet is defending his practice because it is in complete harmony with Old Testament standards. He had not in any way disregarded the Sabbath!

This observation is of the highest significance in our day. It is important because some breathe the spirit of the Pharisees and would reintroduce their stern demands within the modern church. However, even more shocking than those who wish to reconstruct a Pharisaical attitude toward the Sabbath are those who wish to abolish the Sabbath in our day. These people suggest that the Pharisees were right, not Jesus. They try to persuade us that if one day in seven must be kept holy to the Lord, it is inevitable that we will take up the Pharisees' way of doing so! They imply or declare that the only possible way to keep the fourth commandment is in the way of Pharisaical strictness. Their opinion is that the only alternative to the rigidity of the Pharisees is total abolition of the day. Such a position leads to the conclusion that the Pharisees were correct in accusing our Lord and his disciples of Sabbath-breaking. This approach toward rescinding the fourth commandment is an intolerable sacrilege! Jesus' pattern of behaviour is in full compliance with the Sabbath law.

One of the prominent mistakes of the Pharisees was their belief that a day of rest was for the purpose of the fullest possible inactivity and non-exertion. This misconception led the Pharisees to invent a great host of rules as to how much weight a person might pick up, or how far he might walk on the Sabbath. It was this fallacy in their understanding which led them to accuse the disciples of working when they picked grain to relieve their hunger (*verses 1–2*). It was this that led them to misconstrue Jesus' healing as being forbidden work (*verses 9–10*). It was this that so angered the Pharisees when they saw a recently healed invalid carrying the mat upon which he had been lying (*John 5:1–10*).

Non-effort has never been the great point of the Sabbath. It is not a day for human dormancy or repose in which you are to become passive. If it were as the Pharisees conceived of it, the best Sabbath-keeper would be the one who assumed the most complete state of inertia! Jesus exposed this error of the Pharisees by advocating and defending three types of activity on the Sabbath. In Matthew twelve he boldly asserted that three types of energetic work have always been appropriate on the Sabbath. This had even been true in the Mosaic era with all of its judicial restraints.

The most obvious category of human effort on the Sabbath which our Saviour defended was *works of piety*. The only reason for our resting from our normal employments on the Lord's Day is to redirect our efforts toward the *work* of worshipping and serving the Lord with all of our hearts. John 5:17 records the words of our Lord on another occasion when some Pharisees persecuted him for healing on the Sabbath. He said, 'My Father is always at his work to this very day, and I, too, am working.' The Pharisees had not understood that when God rested from the work of creation, he had not become inactive. Even on the Sabbath he kept up the work of providence, upholding all things by the Word of his power.

On this occasion (of his disciples picking grain on the Sabbath) Jesus asked, 'Haven't you read in the Law that on the Sabbath the priests in the temple desecrate the day, yet are innocent?' (*Matthew 12:5*). When did a priest in the temple work harder than on a Sabbath? On this day he sang praises, offered more sacrifices than on any other day and taught the people. It was because his energies were poured out in the Lord's worship and service that a priest was innocent. If the day is viewed only as one of rest from activity, the priests were the chief profaners of the Sabbath! But such a conclusion would be absurd. Work done in the performance of worship is legitimate. More than that, it is the main intent of the Sabbath Day.

Our Lord also defended *works of necessity*. The twelve apostles were employed in serving Jesus Christ the Son of God. Verse 8 reminds us that he is Lord of the Sabbath. Verse 6 notes that he is greater than the temple. If it were legitimate for priests to work in the service of the temple, much more was any labour appropriate which served the One who fulfilled all the temple's imagery. But even apart from that, the twelve were hungry. Human beings who give themselves to the worship of God have ordinary necessities which should be attended to on the Sabbaths as on other days. Meeting the human needs for food, sleep and cleanliness are in full accord with Sabbath rest. A failure to meet these necessities will distract from worship and service to God.

A third type of work on the Sabbath Day which our Lord endorsed as fully acceptable in Old Testament law is *works of mercy*. Perhaps this was the point at which he had the most conflict with the Pharisees. Jesus had an extensive healing ministry. Often he performed miracles of healing on Sabbath Days. These actions were considered by the Pharisees as impious labour and thus as breaking the fourth commandment. It was in connection with this kind of deed, one of kindness to suffering men, that Jesus asserted, 'It is lawful to do good on the Sabbath' (*Matthew 12:12*). Intentionally the Messiah defied the Pharisees by healing the handicapped before their eyes on the Sabbath Day.

In one sense Jesus' controversy with the Pharisees had to do with narrowness and broadness in application of Biblical principles. It had occurred to the Pharisees that 'necessity' should make a difference in the matter of working on the Sabbath. They recognized that if a man were lying at the point of death, it would be legitimate for others to exert themselves to preserve his life. But the disciples would not die if they had nothing to eat for one day. And the man with the disabled hand would survive if Jesus passed him by. The Pharisees even knew that 'if a sheep fell into a pit on the Sabbath' (*Matthew 12:11*) it must be lifted out. This they thought was 'necessity'. Furthermore, they practised certain works in connection with worship, performing circumcisions on the Sabbath (*John 7:22, 23*).

Our Saviour was much more lenient, broad-minded and charitable in applying the issues of necessity, mercy, and piety to Sabbath works. He was far more indulgent of others' actions, as in the case of his hungry disciples, and far more free in his own labours on behalf of others. His confrontations with the Pharisees involved a collision between broad-minded and narrow-minded application of the principles.

When you confront specific questions regarding behaviour on the Sabbath, you will find some issues of application to be obvious, while others are less clear. If you think of the issue of necessity, all will at once recognize that it is proper on the Sabbath for armed forces and police to defend society. It is appropriate for ambulance drivers, nurses and firefighters to work on God's holy day. None will question in these cases. On the other side of the continuum it is altogether clear that the work of athletes, clowns and trinket salesmen is unnecessary on the Sabbath. Some cases are black and white.

However, there is a very large area that leaves uncertainty. What of food service employees who provide meals for students at college or for residents at resorts? Is eating not necessary on the Sabbath? What of employment at electric generating plants which provide power to hospitals, churches and homes of the elderly? It is impossible to cool down the blast furnace of a steel factory for only one day. Is it necessary work to tend to this part of our industrial complex? Pharisees may have a ready answer, but our Lord Jesus was more liberal in his approach. Great caution must be used.

Pharisees in their use of the categories of piety, necessity and mercy showed very little concern for mankind. They had more pity for the cattle on their farms than for the people in their cities. Their rigidity in applying the Sabbath law demonstrated that they had no compassion for man. Eventually they were ruthless in compelling people to comply with the rules. If it caused human beings enormous pain and inconvenience, that did not disturb the Pharisees. Man would be forced into the Sabbath mould if his head must be cut off to do so!

In Mark's account of this incident of the disciples' publicly picking their lunch from a garden on the Sabbath, some of Jesus' words are given which Matthew's account omits. 'The Sabbath was made for man, not man for the Sabbath' (*Mark 2:27*). In other words, the Sabbath was made for man's welfare. It was always designed for man's good. Never did the Lord intend that man suffer to promote the Sabbath. When interpretations of the fourth commandment become so unreasonable that they force us through painful contortions which ignore our own well-being, the interpreter must be mistaken. Pharisees, ancient and modern, discredit the law they pretend to support. The Sabbath was made for the good of man.

A disregard for our fellow-man in applying the Sabbath law comes into existence today as it did with ancient Pharisees. There is a self-admiration in every fallen heart which shows itself by being strict with others but lenient with oneself. As we have seen, Pharisees thought it quite proper for them to lift a sheep out of a pit on God's holy day, but Jesus could not heal the man with a withered hand. Pharisees could circumsise on the Sabbath, but Jesus was not to lift up the invalid of thirty-eight years, relieving enormous suffering.

In their strictness with others, great attention was given to externals by the Pharisees. In excusing themselves, pure motives were assumed. The very opposite approach is to be taken when we make judgments. Knowing the imperfections of our own motives, we should be slow to justify our own deeds or to exalt them as standards for others. Being able to examine ourselves, we must not assume that our motives are pure. Having no access to the hearts of our brothers, it is our duty to presume that they act with God-fearing motives (*Romans 14:1–12*).

Our Lord Jesus returns our attention to principles and matters of the heart. The Sabbath law was given for man's happiness and well-being. God's blessing of the day was an expression of his intent that man be blessed by the day. It is a day for spiritual worship and service to the Most High. So far as possible, one is to cease from his ordinary labours and cease from employing others so that all may devote the Sabbath Day to the Lord. But this requirement was never intended to apply to matters of necessity and mercy. The day must bring blessing to man and especially to his soul.

4

DOES THE NEW TESTAMENT TEACH
THE FOURTH COMMANDMENT?

Then he said to them, 'The Sabbath was made for man, not man for the Sabbath. So the Son of Man is Lord even of the Sabbath.'

[Mark 2:27, 28]

Many have written and preached that Christians are under no obligation to keep the Sabbath holy. One of the most remarkable lines of reasoning for this position has been the claim that the New Testament is silent on the fourth commandment. 'Anti-Sabbatarians' have said that the New Testament asserts the validity of the other nine commandments as a code of Christian conduct but says nothing about the fourth.

This assertion cannot stand in the light of many passages whose leading topic is the Sabbath and whose express concern is to teach the continuing validity of this moral requirement. Matthew 12:1–14, Mark 2:23–3:6, Luke 6:1–11, Luke 13:10–17, Luke 14:1–6, John 5:1–18, and John 7:20–24 are found in the *New* Testament (as is Hebrews 4:7–10). They contain our Lord Jesus' frequent and extensive teaching on the subject. His comments in these places are a rather thorough clarification of the fourth commandment. In his public ministry our Lord gave considerable time and effort to an exposition of the Sabbath issue.

If anyone says that the New Testament does not teach the fourth commandment, perhaps he should read the Gospels before he pretends to speak for the whole Testament. However, if the erroneous nature of such a claim is pointed out to the one making it, he is likely to respond, 'Oh, Jesus was only speaking to the Jews!' Such a response calls our attention to one of the great difficulties which arises when modern evangelicals discuss the Bible and its teaching.

In the United States, the Bible School movement and the Scofield Bible have spread far and wide a system of thought called 'dispensationalism'. Dispensationalism is a theology which distorts one's understanding of Scripture and places blinders on Bible students. Already, in the opening paragraphs of this chapter, we have expressed two of its leading principles from the mouths of those who deny that the Sabbath is to be observed by Christians.

It is dispensationalism which has given the popular impression that a Christian may dismiss any Old Testament teaching or commandment unless it is also repeated in the New Testament. A more unsound principle for interpreting the Bible cannot be imagined. Under such a premise Christians would lose large portions of the Psalms and the wise directives of Proverbs never repeated in the New Testament. Yet many who would be horrified at losing such a great portion of sacred Scripture will be shaken and made to think twice by the (false) accusation that the New Testament does not teach the Sabbath.

Dispensationalism is also the culprit which has taught that the Jews and the Christian church have virtually nothing to do with each other. It is the opinion of dispensationalists that Jesus came to earth as the Messiah of the Jews. He appealed to them to accept him as Messiah, these teachers tell us, but when he was rejected, Jesus became Lord of the church only until he could complete his original mission to the Jews. The tendency of this outlook is to assert that much of Jesus' teachings is intended for the Jewish people and not for the church. Some have taken from Christians the entire Sermon on the Mount, claiming that it had only Jewish reference. A few have further divided Scriptures, telling us that the Gospel instructions are for Jews alone. Christians are to heed only those things taught in the apostolic epistles.

This is precisely the meaning of those who deny that the Sabbath has been taught in the New Testament. Gospel accounts of the Saviour teaching on the subject again and again may be considered irrelevant, they would say. You must find the Sabbath command reissued in the epistles or it is uniquely Jewish. Anyone impressed with such theology and its arguments has been left with a very small Bible. He does not even have an entire New Testament. Genesis through John are Jewish. Acts through Revelation are Christian. Such is the implication of all teaching which draws such strict boundaries between Judaism and Christianity, between Old Testament and New. It is a viewpoint which cannot be defended.

A dispensational treatment of the Sabbath (as outlined above) simply cannot stand in the presence of Jesus' teaching. Especially is this true of our Lord's words, 'The Sabbath was made for man, not man for the Sabbath. So the Son of Man is Lord even of the Sabbath' (*Mark 2:27, 28*). This statement forcefully contradicts those who, with preconceived bias, expect to find the Sabbath rescinded in the New Testament era.

Jesus begins by pointing us back to the 'making' of

the Sabbath. His words do *not* carry us back to the formation of Judaism. If he were to have believed that the Sabbath was merely part of a Jewish legalistic system, we would expect that the formation of the Sabbath would come at the time of the establishment of Judaism. That, however, is not the case.

The formula with which Jesus speaks compels us to think about the creation week. It was then that man was made on the sixth day. It was also then that the Sabbath was made on the seventh day. From the order in which man and Sabbath were created, our Lord determines which was intended to serve the interest of the other. Since man was created before the Sabbath was made we must conclude that the Sabbath was made to serve man's well-being. Man was not made to be subordinated to the interests of the Sabbath. The Sabbath was intended for man's help and welfare.

Paul uses almost an identical formula in 1 Corinthians 11:8–9. 'Man did not come from woman, but woman from man; neither was man created for woman but woman for man.' The order of creation illustrates the divine intent that woman was to be a help suited for him. In the same way our Lord argues that the Sabbath was made to serve man and its interests are to be subordinated to man's.

Our Saviour and Teacher clearly understood that 'the Sabbath was made' at creation, not at the institution of the Mosaic covenant or the Abrahamic arrangement. It was on the seventh day of creation week that God made the day holy (*Genesis 2:3*). It was also on the seventh day of creation week that God blessed the seventh day (*Genesis 2:3*). At creation week he revealed that it would bring blessing to man. This declaration or promise is akin to stating that the

Sabbath was made for man. It was not simply a rest that God observed. The Lord instituted the Sabbath for man's happiness and welfare at the time of creation!

Furthermore, it is evident that when at creation week God made the Sabbath for man, his reference was not to Jewish man alone. It was for Adam and all his posterity that the Sabbath was made. Sabbath was made to be profitable for all mankind. Anyone without preconceived prejudice and a passion to defend a theological quirk will see the obvious meaning of Jesus' comment. The Sabbath was made for the enrichment of all mankind at the time of creation. These things are made clear in the order of creation and in specific divine statements interpreting creation activity.

Anyone who claims that the Sabbath is uniquely Jewish is arguing against Moses, the founding prophet of Judaism, who wrote Genesis. He is also plainly contradicting the express teaching of our Lord Jesus Christ. It is simply not a defensible position. It is not the Bible's position in either the Old Testament or the New. It is true that Jesus was speaking to Jews in Mark 2 and other Gospel passages. But he was not discussing a matter unique to Jewish ceremony or Jewish law. The Sabbath is an issue of morality which touches all mankind from the time of creation.

In this same statement of Mark 2:27, 28, our Lord Jesus intimates the continuing importance of the Sabbath. 'So the Son of Man is Lord even of the Sabbath.' The word translated 'so' by the NIV is translated 'therefore' in the KJV and 'so that' by still others. The word connects the thoughts of the two sentences of verses 27 and 28. Since at creation the Sabbath was made for the benefit of all mankind and man was not made to be sacrificed in the interests of the

Sabbath, therefore the Son of Man is Lord even of the Sabbath. What was made for the improvement of mankind is taken under the dominion of the Son of Man. He has become Lord of the Sabbath Day.

Those who teach that Christians need not keep the Sabbath holy to the Lord dismiss these words by suggesting that Jesus became Lord of the Sabbath in order to abolish it. He became Lord of the Sabbath, used his public ministry to teach extensively on the Sabbath, and after a few short months eradicated the Sabbath. Such is their contention.

There are three serious problems with this line of reasoning. First, it makes nonsense of Jesus' words themselves. The sense given by those who claim that Jesus removed the Sabbath institution is as follows: 'Since from the very time of creation God made the Sabbath to be a blessing for all mankind, therefore the Son of Man will become Lord of this blessing to demolish it. Never again will man have to endure the Sabbath.' Only those who view the Sabbath as a burden, not a blessing, could possibly speak in this fashion. Dispensational prejudice, by its interpretations, makes our Lord's words self-contradictory. He has said that the Sabbath is good for man!

A second serious problem with teaching that Jesus became Lord of the Sabbath for a few years only to abolish it is the incongruity of this thought with the rest of the New Testament. Galatians 4:4 tells us that 'God sent his Son, born of a woman, born *under* law, to redeem those under law.' There were indeed ceremonial and judicial laws from which man had to be delivered. This code of regulations 'he took . . . away, nailing it to the cross' (*Colossians 2:14*). He destroyed this barrier (*Ephesians 2:14, 15*). But always our Lord is pictured as subject to the law and nailed to the cross with the law. Never does the Scripture speak of his becoming Lord of a law to dismiss a law.

Thirdly, our Lord Jesus selects the title 'Son of Man' for himself in connection with becoming Lord of the Sabbath. The Son of Man is a title for the Messiah taken from the prophet Daniel. In the Book of Daniel great emphasis is given to the successive empires of brutal Gentile nations ruling the earth. One cruel empire after another dominates the world until the Son of Man comes. He ushers in a new order of grace and glory. His kingdom shall never end. Unlike the rule of conquering world powers, the Son of Man is to establish a reign which includes all that is good and blessed for mankind. It will be a universal (not Jewish) kingdom. In Mark 2:27–28 the Lord Jesus is saying that the Son of Man takes up the Sabbath into his great kingdom because it is one of the institutions which has benefitted man since the creation of the world. His is the kingdom which will fill the whole earth, gathering in Gentiles as well as Jews. In this kingdom, the Sabbath must have a place; for it serves the best interests of mankind.

Behind much of the passion to eliminate Sabbath Days from the church of Jesus Christ is the unbiblical dispensational assumption that there is a fundamental difference between Old Testament religion and Christianity. Dispensationalism proposes that Israel and the church have nothing to do with one another and must be kept utterly separate to understand the Bible.

That such a teaching is completely false may be seen by a careful reading of a few New Testament passages. Ephesus was a largely Gentile church. In writing to the

Ephesians Paul said, 'Remember, that formerly you who are Gentiles by birth and called "uncircumcised" by those who call themselves "the circumcision" . . . remember that at that time you were separate from Christ, excluded from citizenship in Israel and for-eigners to the covenants of promise' (*Ephesians 2:11–12*). That was the situation in Old Testament times. But what is the position of believing Gentiles now? Paul goes on: 'But now in Christ Jesus you who once were far away have been brought near through the blood of Christ. For he himself is our peace, who has made the two one . . . His purpose was to create in himself one new man out of the two . . . in this one body . . . you are . . . fellow citizens with God's people and members of God's household . . . joined together . . . built together . . .' (*Ephesians 2:13–22*).

Paul did not believe that the Gentile church and Israel were separate entities. In Christ Israel and the church had been fused into one body. That is why he calls the church 'the Israel of God' (*Galatians 6:16*). The church has 'come to Mount Zion, to the heavenly Jerusalem' (*Hebrews 12:22*). Jesus Christ has put a decisive end to the separation of Jew and Gentile. He has a unified and universal kingdom. The church is the spiritual Israel, both Jew and Gentile.

Israel and the church publish an identical way of salvation for sinners. It is by grace alone through faith alone in Jesus the Christ alone. Never did either Israel or the church propose any other way for sinners to be right with God. Furthermore, Israel and the church have always agreed on their definition of sin. 'Sin is the transgression of the law' (*1 John 3:4*). 'By the law is the knowledge of sin' (*Romans 3:20*). There is but one moral law for Israel and the church, the Ten

Commandments, given at Mount Sinai. In the midst of the ten is the command, 'Remember the Sabbath day by keeping it holy' (*Exodus 20:8*). Never in Israel or the church did the gospel of salvation by grace through faith promote lawlessness. In Old Testament and New men and women of faith were 'created in Christ Jesus to do good works' (*Ephesians 2:10*). Salvation appeared both to Israel and to the church to teach us 'to live self-controlled, upright and godly lives in this present age' (*Titus 2:11–12*). That involved for Israel and the church the fourth commandment.

5

SABBATH OBSERVANCE: MOSAIC AND CHRISTIAN

While the Israelites were in the desert, a man was found gathering wood on the Sabbath day. Those who found him gathering wood brought him to Moses and Aaron and the whole assembly, and they kept him in custody, because it was not clear what should be done to him. Then the LORD said to Moses, 'The man must die. The whole assembly must stone him outside the camp.' So the assembly took him outside the camp and stoned him to death, as the LORD commanded Moses.

[Numbers 15:32–36]

Men of Tyre who lived in Jerusalem were bringing in fish and all kinds of merchandise and selling them in Jerusalem on the Sabbath to the people of Judah . . . I warned them and said . . . 'If you do this again, I will lay hands on you' (Nehemiah 13:16, 21).

We were held prisoners by the law, locked up until faith should be revealed . . . Now that faith has come, we are no longer under the supervision of the law (Galatians 3:23, 25).

During the lifetime of Moses a man gathered wood in the desert on the Sabbath Day. Almighty God personally commanded that the Sabbath-breaker be stoned. Obeying the directive from Jehovah, the assembly of Jews stoned him to death. Jewish Sabbath practice was very strict. The State of Israel enforced the fourth commandment with capital punishment. Not only did the people watch the execution. They were all executioners.

Nehemiah was very jealous for public righteousness. In his zeal for Sabbath-keeping he threatened merchants with personal physical assault if they continued to break God's law. To know what Nehemiah had in mind, we need only look at his actions toward those who intermarried with heathen. 'I rebuked them and called curses down on them. I beat some of the men and pulled out their hair' (*Nehemiah 13:25*). It was terrifying to confront Nehemiah or any Jewish magistrate when he was outraged over moral issues.

As the Sabbath was practised under Moses, the fourth commandment was rigorously applied and any offence was met with severe punishment. Moses' system was exacting, stern, unyielding and stark. That is why Peter, who lived under the Mosaic covenant, said, 'Neither we nor our fathers have been able to bear' the law of Moses (*Acts 15:10*). That is why Paul, the super-strict Pharisee, said, 'We were held prisoners by the law, locked up . . .' (*Galatians 3:23*).

There are two unbiblical responses to the rigorous and imperious style of administering God's law under Moses. Some modern day students of the Bible look at the ethical chaos all around us. In the face of collapsing morals, of utter disregard for righteousness, these believe that only Mosaic austerity could possible restore public morality. Others are so horrified at the thought of returning to the inflexible ways of Mosaic culture that they wish to cut off the Old Testament entirely. These see nothing worth preserving in Old Testament law. Neither is the New Testament position.

Galatians 3:6–4:7 gives us quite a different outlook

from these two growing reactions toward the Mosaic system. This perspective is vital to understanding how the fourth commandment is to be understood and applied in our day.

First, the New Testament never abandons the moral law revealed in the Old Testament. God is righteous. He demands that man be righteous just like himself if man is to receive God's favour, communion and blessing. When our Lord Jesus and his disciples define moral purity, they rely entirely upon Old Testament Scriptures for their definitions. They return over and over again to the Ten Commandments, quoting them and alluding to them. Furthermore, this moral law is essential to defining our gospel, and the gospel has never changed from the days of Adam, or Noah, or Abraham, or Moses, or David, to Christ. Always men have been made righteous by faith in the Messiah. Keeping the Sabbath Day holy is a commandment embedded in the code of moral law written by God's own finger. It is part of the definition of righteousness.

However, the moral law in the hands of Moses was wielded quite differently from the same law in the hands of Jesus Christ. Precisely the same standard of morality is found in the covenant of Moses and in the New Covenant. Yet the administration of this moral law is widely different. The ways in which the moral law was applied and the ways in which it was enforced differ greatly when we compare the management of Moses and the management of Christ.

When Moses, under inspiration, superintended the law he taught its application by giving very exact external details for living. Sticks must not be gathered on the Sabbath (*Numbers 15:32–36*). No fire must be lit in their dwellings (*Exodus 35:3*) on the Sabbath. Additional sacrifices were prescribed for the Sabbath day (*Numbers 28:9–10*). Strict instructions down to minute particulars were given.

Our Saviour handled precisely the same Sabbath law in a different spirit. He elucidated the principles involved in the Sabbath commandment, emphasizing inward matters of heart motives. He displayed a much greater disposition of leniency, granting men a larger freedom. This we observed both in his tolerance of his disciples' picking grain on the Sabbath and in his teaching on that occasion.

When someone broke the Sabbath under Moses' economy there was a clearly-defined response from the state. 'Whoever does any work on it (the Sabbath) must be put to death' (*Exodus 35:2*). When narrowly defined lines were crossed, the offender was met with stiff and unsparing punishment. Moses was unrelenting in application of the moral law in external civil affairs.

Again one must note the contrast in our Lord Jesus' managing of moral issues. He fully upheld the moral law, convincing the conscience of offences against the commandments within the thoughts and intents of the soul and when words were spoken injudiciously. The Master reminds us of God's judgment but stipulates no civil reprisals for breaking the Sabbath.

This same contrast may be seen as the two Mediators handle others of God's moral laws. Moses elaborates endlessly on the external details of obedience. Punishments abound. For a sorceress – death; for bestiality – death; for idolatry – death; for a priest's daughter who becomes a prostitute – death by burning; for adultery – death. When our Saviour takes up the law, he too enforces it but always by spiritual exposition and without dictating severe civil punishments. Both Moses and Jesus are faithful to the Ten Commandments but they administer that law with widely different styles.

In Galatians 3 and 4 Paul gives us a clear explanation of the difference between the covenant of Moses and the New Covenant instituted by Jesus Christ. This comparison of the two religious systems has important bearing for our understanding of, and practice under, the fourth commandment.

Jesus' New Covenant was not a completely new beginning. God did not send his Son to rescind all former covenants. Messiah did not entirely demolish the Old Testament and start afresh. He and his disciples stood upon the Old Testament and used it to argue the rightness of their position. Never is there a hint that one should reject the old unless its teaching is repeated in the new.

Paul shows us, for instance, that all of the Old Testament, including Moses' writings, taught that there is only one way of salvation. That is Paul's point early on in Galatians 3. 'Consider Abraham: "He believed God, and it was credited to him as righteousness"' (*verse 6*). 'Clearly no one is justified before God by the law, because, "The righteous will live by faith"' (*verse 11*). Paul is quoting Moses in Genesis and Habakkuk, a prophet under the Mosaic order. It was completely clear to Moses and to all Mosaic prophets that no part of the law was intended to show the way of salvation. The Sabbath law never was designed to be part of the way sinners were to come to God for acceptance.

This really is the greatest emphasis of Paul's teaching. The promise of salvation for sinners by grace through faith in the Messiah was given by God to Abraham 430 years before Moses published the covenant of law

(*Galatians 3:17*). Therefore, Moses' law does not and could not set aside that arrangement with Abraham (*Galatians 3:17b*). Moses law did not and *could* not propose a different way of salvation.

At verse 19 of chapter 3 Paul asks, 'What, then, was the purpose of the law?' Even as he answers this question Paul repeats his former insistence, 'Is the law, therefore, opposed to the promises of God? Absolutely not! For if a law had been given that could impart life, then righteousness would certainly have come by the law. But the Scripture (Old Testament) declares that the whole world is a prisoner of sin, so that what was promised, being given through faith in Jesus Christ, might be given to those who believe' (*Galatians 3:21, 22*).

Still, 'What, then, *was* the purpose of the law?' (of Moses). In verse 19 of chapter 3 Paul begins his answer. 'It was added because of transgressions.' Moses' covenant did not replace Abraham's covenant. That was left intact. But Moses' system of law was 'added' to the existing promise of grace. The addition was made because of 'transgressions'. God's moral law was so flagrantly despised by all the heathen nations surrounding the people of God that 'transgressions' threatened to swallow up even the Jews before Messiah came. So much sin remained in their own hearts that the libertine practices of the godless threatened to sweep away all vestiges of a people of God. And this nearly happened at numerous times.

A strict and explicitly detailed application of the commandments joined with austere civil punishments – all under Moses – would preserve the people of God until Messiah came. Paul likened the Hebrews (in Galatians 4) to a young child who is heir of a great estate.

All belongs to him by right, but while he is immature he must be committed to strict schoolmasters – often slaves in the ancient world. The Jews of the Old Testament were like such young children, while the Christian is like an heir come to full age. Slaves no longer administer strict discipline to heirs when they have come to full maturity.

Paul's illustration is further explained in the passage. The Old Testament Jews were small children for two reasons. They did not have the fullness of revelation we Christians have (*3:23–25*).[1] And they did not have the fullness of the Spirit which we Christians have (*4:6–7*). Both of these elements of maturity, the fullness of revelation and the fullness of the indwelling Spirit, were brought to God's people at the coming of Messiah. Thus the Jews could not be treated as fully grown sons, even though they had true faith. Moses' law-covenant was appropriate supervision for children. It is not appropriate for mature children of God.

When a small child lacks all of the information needed for his own safety and lacks the insight to grasp

[1] Paul says that Jews were held prisoners by the law 'before this faith came'. He also writes that 'Now that faith has come' we are no longer under the supervision of the law. He speaks of 'faith' that had not come in Old Testament times but had come in New Testament times. What is this 'faith'? The Bible word 'faith' may be understood subjectively as the faith which people have in their hearts. However, the very same word 'faith' must sometimes be taken objectively, meaning the doctrine or body of truth in which belief is placed. In Galatians 3 Paul has already gone to great pains to show us that subjective faith existed in Abraham 430 years before Moses lived and taught. Therefore, verses 23–25 cannot be understood as teaching that Moses' law held people prisoners before subjective faith came. People believed unto salvation before and during Moses' covenant. It can only mean the full revelation of truth which came with Jesus Christ. 'Faith' in these verses has reference to 'the faith that was once for all entrusted to the saints' (*Jude 3*). The content of faith or the object in which we believe must be in view.

information even when it is given to him, how do we guide him? We do it by repetition of strict outward limits and by threats of painful punishment! If you were the parent of a toddler and you lived near a lake, you would have to be concerned lest he drown. Therefore, you would constantly remind him not to go beyond the treeline unless attended by parents. Not only would you say, 'Don't go into the water.' You would have to be more strict to be safe. 'Do not go onto the beach or the dock without mother and father,' you would say. If at *any* time and for *any* reason he put one foot on the dock or the beach, immediate punishment would result – he would get a spanking. You are preserving his *life*.

That is exactly what God did with the Jews under Moses. They did not have the teaching of Christ or the full revelation of Christ himself. If they did have it, they would not have understood, because they did not have the fullness of the Spirit. Therefore, by judicial and ceremonial additions to the moral law, Jehovah guarded his under-age children from self-destruction through the transgressions so pervasive all around them. The Jews were locked up like prisoners under Mosaic law. It was the only way to preserve them.

When your child is grown to manhood, you will still want to remind him of water safety, perhaps if storms are approaching. You do not want him to perish in the lake in his manhood. But now you speak to him in broad principles, giving him liberty. Extra-strict limits and spankings are completely inappropriate for the mature.

Every Christian should be appalled at moral transgressions in the new heathenism of Western society. All sensitivity to the Sabbath day is rapidly disappearing in our land. People have no time for their God! His holy day is being trampled.

In such a desperate circumstance there is often the temptation to return to Moses. This is done when some stern moralist in the church appoints himself the enforcer of the law. He may frown his disapproval of others' conduct on the Sabbath. He may praise the rigid ways of old Puritan culture or identify with the social patterns of the Scottish Highlands in another era. He may with dour looks and authoritative tone insist that his own decisions on Sabbath practice are the only right ones. 'We must be more strict, more exact than the law itself', his whole bearing says.

Still others believe that all of Moses' rules and punishments must be reintroduced by magistrates. These believe there is no distinction between judicial and moral laws, even though by such beliefs they contradict all the historic Reformed creeds. Sabbath laws should be just as written by Moses and offenders dealt with as in the Pentateuch, they say.

It is obvious that Christ and Peter and Paul are of another opinion. Supervision appropriate to a small child is *not* acceptable for treatment of an adult son! Christians have the full revelation and full measure of the Spirit brought by Christ. On the Sabbath issue as in all moral laws Christ's Spirit must prevail. Neither the strictness nor the rod of Moses may be carried from the Old Testament to the New. Moral law must be preserved. Judicial law must be laid aside.

It is equally frustrating, however, to hear teachers who insist that we abandon the moral law along with the judicial and ceremonial. Because we do not insist on capital punishment for adulterers, must there no longer be any civil sanctions against unchastity and marital unfaithfulness? Because we do not execute idolaters, must we cancel the second commandment? Our Saviour frequently gave spiritual, New Testament exposition of the fourth commandment. Keeping the Sabbath holy is a basic moral obligation. Men and women with the fullness of the Spirit and the fullness of a completed Biblical revelation must be given the moral law as adults. They must hear the principles of Sabbath-keeping without the judicial addenda and the strict flavour of Moses. Still, their liberty as sons of God will be to walk in this commandment in the steps of our Saviour himself. The spiritual essence of the Sabbath may be kept by mature saints without the features of Moses' teaching directed to childish believers.

6

MOTIVES FOR SABBATH-KEEPING

When he came to his senses, he said, 'How many of my father's hired men have food to spare, and here I am starving to death! I will set out and go back to my father and say to him: Father, I have sinned against heaven and against you. I am no longer worthy to be called your son; make me like one of your hired men.' So he got up and went to his father.

[Luke 15:17–20]

The older brother became angry and refused to go in. So his father went out and pleaded with him. But he answered his father, 'Look! All these years I've been slaving for you and never disobeyed your orders. Yet you never gave me even a young goat so I could celebrate with my friends. But when this son of yours who has squandered your property with prostitutes comes home, you kill the fattened calf for him!'

[Luke 15:28–30]

Obedience to God's commands is of major importance to true religion. It was in the Old Testament and it is in the New Covenant. Every Christian will remember Jesus' teaching in the Sermon on the Mount, 'Let your light shine before men that they may see your *good deeds* and praise your Father in heaven' (*Matthew 5:16*). Just before going to the cross, our precious Lord said, 'If you love me, you will obey what I command' (*John 14:15*). Obeying commandments and doing good works are vital to Christianity. That would include the fourth commandment enforced by the

teachings of Christ, and the good work of keeping the
Sabbath Day holy.

Jesus' parable of the Prodigal Son has something to
teach on the subject of obedience which will instruct us
in how to obey the Sabbath commandment. The matter
of obedience is not the major lesson being taught by
this parable. However, there is more than one lesson
being imparted in Jesus' remarkable story. Attitudes
toward obedience are very obvious in this tale. Three
different moods related to good works surface in the
parable.

Behind the younger son's request for his share of the
inheritance was an unwillingness to live by the rules of
his father's house. This young man was eager to be free
from all restraints, free to disobey his father and to
abandon his standard of morality. We recognize in this
picture the mind-set of the ungodly worldling. He
hates God's law, and loathes the restrictive demand
that one day in each seven must be given to the Lord.
Although God has created the disobedient person and
showered upon him earthly riches, the rebellious
sinner wishes to depart far from the commandments.
In a far country (far from God) he may forget God's
rules and live in disregard of them. Such a frame of
mind is a major element in the spirit of our age which
rejects and ignores the fourth commandment.

An opposite frame of heart toward good works is
displayed in the same younger son. This second
attitude toward obedience developed in the distress of
tasting bitter consequences from sin and the selfish
insensitivity of worldly 'friends'. In loneliness and
want the prodigal began to think of service in his
father's household. Then he realized that his father's
management was fair and good for all who worked

under him. At that time he realized that it was desirable to live under the wise rules of his father. This wayward son knew that he could never deserve the privilege of living with and working for his father. He had grievously sinned. But he also knew his father to be a gracious and kind man. He therefore resolved to go to him and to ask to be taken on as the lowest servant of the household. He had now begun to desire the good life of doing his father's will.

Our imagination carries us beyond the joyful celebration at the return of the younger son. If the prodigal was willing to obey and work for his father as a hired man in order to have a warm bed in which to sleep and bread to eat, how must his heart have leaped to serve the father after the fattened calf was killed and the high honour of sonship was restored to him! What grateful, loving, hearty obedience he would resolve to give to the father.

This second state of feelings toward God's commandments should characterize every true Christian during his conversion experience and ever after. In the painful and sorrowful experiences of the hard consequences of our own transgressions, our minds should think high thoughts of the goodness of God's kingdom and rule. His commands are after all in the best interest of those who obey them. What joyful and abundant benefits flow from Sabbath-keeping! Did you not at conversion pledge to keep all the Lord's holy will? Did this not include his moral law and the fourth commandment?

After tasting the exquisite generosity of God's grace – not only to pardon our multitude of sins against his law and to admit us again to his service, but also to make us sons and daughters of God, priests and kings with Christ – our hearts should overflow with loving obedience. If it would please him that I kept the Sabbath Day, my heart would run with delight to the task. Oh, to return something to the One who has been infinitely gracious and kind to me! Sabbath observance surely is part of this return of obedience.

In the parable, our Lord Jesus had his eye on the Pharisees. Their disposition toward obedience is shown in the resentment of the older son. The prodigal's brother resented the service he had given his father. His labour for the father was outwardly filled with good deeds, but these works were performed grudgingly. Envy filled his heart at the gracious reception given to a brother whose whole life had been disobedient. 'Surely the external faithfulness of the brother who stayed at home deserved the father's best rewards,' he firmly believed.

Are there not, even in Reformed churches, some who never get drunk, never visit harlots and never break the Sabbath, whose obedience is given in the spirit of the older brother? It is possible to expect to earn the kindness of God by careful Sabbath obedience. Strict adherence to the fourth commandment may seem hard and difficult to modern Pharisees, but necessary, they would think, to win God's smile. They slave for God to keep the day holy, and are dismayed over the question of how God could possibly bless Sabbath-breakers more than Sabbath-keepers.

In the story, we have the disobedient evil works of the unreligious, the obedient good works of the converted sinner, and the externally obedient good works of the self-righteous which really turn out to be evil deeds because of their improper motives. At least the disobedient *know* that they have transgressed

God's law, whether they regret it or not. For this reason harlots and publicans enter God's kingdom sooner than do Pharisees who are unaware of their guilt and their need of a Saviour. It is only the genuinely converted sinner who has fresh resolves to obey the Lord from his heart. Sinners, conscious of the enormous mercy of God to them in making them children of God and feeling the kiss of reconciliation, are zealous to do good works.

Saddest of all God's creatures in the world is the religious person who has disciplined himself to outward obedience but who has no inward love to God. He seems to be a good person. He has worked long and hard to keep God's commandments. He has toiled and sacrificed to obey, but his heart is not right with God. Alas, his obedience is empty, useless and worse than the disobedience of the ungodly.

At least one striking contrast in the parable is this: The obedience of the penitent son is 'evangelical', but the obedience of the older brother is 'legal'. Any time the Christian talks about commandments and moral laws and good works he ought to recognize an urgent necessity to keep in mind the distinction between legal obedience and evangelical obedience. Every Christian should evangelically obey the fourth commandment. However, those who yield only legal obedience to God's Sabbath law – and to all other commandments – will perish with the Pharisees.

There is no difference between legal obedience and evangelical obedience so far as outward standards are concerned. The older brother worked long and hard in the service of his father under the rules of the father's management. The returning prodigal pledged himself to the same long and hard labour in the service of his father following his directions and rules. All the distinction between legal and evangelical obedience is to be found in the thoughts and intents of the hearts of those who keep the commandments.

Legal obedience flows from hard thoughts about God, his law, his people. The older brother obeyed the father but thought of him as strict, over-demanding and unappreciative. Although he had done what the father wanted, he felt that the father had not been kind to him. Keeping father's law was like slavery to him. Other sons were undeserving of the favours God heaped upon them because they had not been so externally strict as he had been. He looked down upon younger brother.

Evangelical obedience arises from tender thoughts toward God, his law, his people. The repentant prodigal had warm and loving thoughts of his father. How pleasant it had become to work for him. He knew now that his father's goodness abounded to all. He wanted to be at home and under the father's rules. They were a delight to him. Far from having negative thoughts toward other sons, the wayward man thought of *himself* as unworthy to be included in the family. He should be considered the least of all those who did good works. He was delighted to be considered for last place.

At the very heart of the distinction is how the legal servant and the evangelical servant conceived of the function of their service. Why did they do their good works? What role did obedience play in their personal relationships with the father? What purpose did good works serve?

You will notice why the older son obeyed his father. He expected to earn the favour and blessing of the father through the works he performed. He thought that careful, sacrificial obedience would win the father's love and purchase his inheritance. When an impressive array of good works failed to make him the father's favourite, he was angry, envious and rude to his father. Because of this misunderstanding of the appropriate role of good works he became more and more strict, out of fear that he would miss the blessing. When the older brother compared himself to the younger in conversation with his father, he sounded exactly like the Pharisee in the temple in Luke 18:10–12. This attitude is the essence of legal obedience.

Quite opposite was the motive and goal of the penitent son. Recognizing himself as altogether unworthy of the father's acceptance and love, the younger son knew of no good works that he could do to reinstate himself in the good graces of his father. He had in the past squandered a wonderful opportunity. His sincere conviction of sin forever delivered him from the false hope that his good works would win God's favour and blessing. He approached the father hoping only in his father's mercy and kindness which he knew were always abundantly bestowed on the undeserving. He decided simply to beg for mercy.

Still, the younger son never imagined that he would receive mercy from the father without a pledge of humble obedience. He could not carry his harlots and wine into his father's presence and ask for mercy. There was in his heart a new resolve to obey the father. There is no hint that the father was expected to cancel all commandments as if they had been the reasons for the son's disobedience. The commandments were the very expression of the father's personal character and will.

The prodigal had lived by the rules of the world and had found them cruel and unfair. The father's laws were righteous and good. In repentance, the younger son approved of and endorsed the commandments of the father. He would rather be a doorkeeper in his father's house than dwell in the tents of the wicked. He had no complaints against his father's management. The ways of the transgressor are hard, not the ways of the father.

Upon returning, the wicked son discovered that the father did not wait for him to work before receiving him. He was embraced and honoured and made a son with loving enthusiasm without prior obedience from him. How then do you think he served the father and obeyed his rules? A grateful heart cried, 'What can I do to show appreciation for mercy shown to me?' Evangelical obedience is keeping the commandments out of gratitude for kindnesses God has already given! Thankful love is not seeking to secure God's favour by good works. It is attempting to give something back to God for his great mercies already received. Yet in such an endeavour, it is the same moral laws that are evangelically obeyed.

God's fourth commandment is that we are to remember the Sabbath Day by keeping it holy. On the Sabbath we are not to do any work or to employ others to work for us. It is a miserable and hopeless business to obey this commandment with the goal of securing God's love and favour by doing so. It will become a source of anger and envy if you hope to win the love of God by keeping the Sabbath. If you expect to climb to a higher position in God's appreciation by Sabbath observance you are apt to experience frustration and dismay. The Sabbath will be no delight to you if you keep it out of fear that God will do dreadful things to you if you do not comply with his law.

It is in fear of such motives creeping into Christian hearts as they obey that antinomians (those who are 'against law') want to eradicate the Ten Commandments. They are correct in wanting to avoid all legal motives. However, their suspicion is that the law always produces legal motives. That is not true, as the younger son shows us.

Every genuine believer will delight in the law of God in the inward man. He ought to run in the way of the fourth commandment as a delight. Forgiven sinners have received such unbelievably precious gifts from God's hand, by grace through Christ, that they are eager to do something for him. Christians are delighted to keep the Sabbath holy. Sabbath Days bring them nearer still to the God they love and who loves them. Their love wants to give obedience and honour to the Lord on his day.

Ministers of the gospel rightly become alarmed at the lawlessness of our age. There is even a brand of professed Christianity which has no holiness of life attached to it. Our world is under the dominion of the wicked one. Believers are ignorant of how to obey God. In this atmosphere there are temptations to give an overdose of commandments in preaching.

When severe denunciations of sin and warnings of judgment begin to dominate the pulpit, Christians may unconsciously slip into the frame of mind of the older brother. Legal attitudes creep in. 'I must obey or God will be angry with me,' people think under much law preaching. 'I must be good to win his blessing. I must obey the Sabbath or else!' They should be motivated to obedience by an awareness that God has loved them when they were undeserving of his tender mercies.

The younger brother's obedience flowed from pleasant memories of the goodness and kindness of his father. Upon his return, the prodigal spent moments in the arms of his father *before* he went to work. Precious and tender things were spoken to him in a loving embrace. The younger brother spent time in exhilarating, joyful celebration as the backdrop to his obedience. Joyful communion with God and delightful worship is a great means of sanctification.

Beware of driving men into the stern attitudes of the older brother. Parents must beware of this with children. There must be an atmosphere of love and kindness and rejoicing in the Lord if children or adults are to want to keep God's law. And if children depart far from God, memories of the happiness of his house will do much to bring them back. Sometimes Reformed churches and Christian homes are too heavy, too strict, too negative about God's law. We must make the Sabbath a delight to our congregations and to our children so that their obedience will be evangelical.

There is with some leaders in our day an impatience with the means of grace and an impatience with relying on the Holy Spirit. Because disobedience to the fourth commandment and to all other moral laws has become so general, there has come a human determination to change things. Because teaching the truth and relying upon the Spirit have not produced a high degree of obedience under modern ministries there is a craving for other measures to compel the church to good works.

Thus, in this day of disregard for the Ten Commandments authoritarian oversight has emerged. Elders are determined to insist that church members keep the Sabbath in detailed specific application. Very specific instructions are given to all members and close watch is kept on their practices. It is then said that with this procedure the elders care for their souls. A rigid, overbearing eldership begins to lord it over the flock regarding the Sabbath and a host of other moral issues. These authoritarian tactics begin to take away the liberty Jesus Christ has given his people. A super-strict oversight returns Christians to a childhood status inappropriate to them now that they have the fullness of revelation and of the Spirit. Interfacing scrutiny and excessive directions from misconceived eldership drives Christians back into a legal obedience, a cheerless, wrong-intentioned pattern of good works.

Reform-minded leaders who wish to teach the Sabbath commandment have need to beware of making 'older brothers' of their people. There is an important balance to be found in teaching the commandments and in stirring up right motives to obey them. The external standard and a proper motive must come together and must be demonstrated in the spirit and with the methods of the teacher of believers as they were in the case of our Lord Jesus himself.

The fourth commandment, as well as the other nine, may be used to convince the godless rebel and the self-righteous moralist of their need for a Saviour. It can indeed demonstrate that neither the worldling nor the Pharisee is worthy to be called God's son. Their one plea must be for mercy. Then, for the repentant sinner, grateful for the warm reception by the Father, the Sabbath law is an important direction to good works of loving service. Although the same law may be used with its same outward demands in many different cases, it is essential for the teacher to be aware of the very different motives of men's hearts. It is necessary that the same Sabbath requirement be handled in various ways according to the differing motives of the ones who hear.

7

WHICH DAY OF THE WEEK IS THE SABBATH?

On the Lord's Day I was in the Spirit.

[Revelation 1:10]

On the first day of the week we came together to break bread.

[Acts 20:7]

On the first day of every week, each one of you should set aside a sum of money in keeping with his income . . . so that when I come no collections will have to be made.

[1 Corinthians 16:2]

There remains then a keeping of a Sabbath for the people of God; for he who did enter his rest did rest from all his works, even as God did from his.

[Hebrews 4:9–10]

Most Christians worship on the first day of the week. Jews worship on the seventh day. Muslims worship on the sixth day. All of this can be very confusing to someone who has just come to realize that he ought to worship God for one day each week. The confusion has even proved to be a stumbling block to older Christians. It may become a reason which some use to abandon the fourth commandment altogether.

Didn't the fourth commandment point back to God's rest at creation? When teaching about the Sabbath didn't our Lord Jesus also point us back to God's creation rest? This was on the seventh day!

From the beginning of the world until the time of Christ everyone who responded to divine revelation by keeping a Sabbath Day holy observed the seventh day. When Christians worship on the first day of the week, have they abandoned God's example? Does their day of worship have anything to do with God's rest at creation? Or have they eliminated the fourth commandment? This is the bewilderment which enters many thinking minds.

Perhaps the easiest step to take is to show that the New Testament saints did worship on the first day of the week after Jesus' resurrection. Our Lord Jesus rose from the dead on the first day. Our Saviour's early appearances to the saints came on the first day. 'On the evening of the first day of the week, when the disciples were together' (*John 20:19*), Jesus first met with the gathered disciples. Thomas was not present on that occasion. Our Lord did not disclose himself to the doubter until the next first day (*John 20:26*). A pattern was being set.

It became the habit of Christians to meet for worship on the first day of the week. This was firmly established in the apostolic era. When Paul wrote to the churches about a special offering for the needy, which he was overseeing, he instructed people to give on the first day of the week (*1 Corinthians 16:1–4*). Churches in Galatia and Corinth were to take their collections on this day because they all met to worship on the first day. When Paul travelled to Jerusalem for the last time and wished to say a personal farewell to believers at Troas, he delayed his journey an entire week so that he could meet with the assembly of saints. It was on the first day that they gathered for worship and Paul wanted to be in their midst (*Acts 20:6–7*).

When the apostle John was exiled to the island of Patmos, God gave a remarkable *Revelation* to him and to us. It was the last of the divinely inspired books. He received his astounding visions 'on the Lord's Day', the day of our Lord Jesus Christ. By this time all Christians understood that the Lord's Day was the day of the Lord's resurrection, the day of the Lord's pouring out of the Spirit, the day Christians everywhere met under the Lord for worship. The Lord of the church universal has a day! It is the first day of the week.

This example of the apostles and of the earliest church is easy to note. However, questions persist. Was the Lord's Day something entirely new, having nothing to do with the Sabbath of the fourth commandment? Did early Christians recognize any obligation to keep an entire day holy, now the first day? Was the fourth commandment to remain in effect but the day of the week for Sabbath observance to change? Would such a change of days, from seventh to first, utterly demolish the fourth commandment? Is seventh day worship so much of the essence of the fourth commandment that abandoning it for first day worship will cause the entire law to crumble and disappear?

Answers to such problems may wind through many long and twisted mountain and valley roads of theology. These paths are often difficult to navigate and they cannot be passed over quickly. Hints and general directions may be given at the start of the way to new travellers on foot. Yet it will require many days of experience and long climbs in thought before the full answer will be known.

All things in Scripture are not equally simple to understand. Some matters are plainly spoken in a proof text. A single verse, all by itself, may settle once and for all the way of salvation. Other issues are not explained with individual verses. Some statements must be understood by careful study of whole chapters of context. The meaning of certain Bible statements may not be understood until they are looked at in the light of many other passages. Immature Christians may grow discouraged with the lengthy process of finding complex answers. They may ask, 'If God wanted me to keep a Sabbath on the first day of the week, wouldn't there be one plain verse saying so? Who has time to study it through?'

Let's put together the facts we already are sure of from previous chapters. God's command to keep an entire day holy each week is embedded in the heart of the Ten Commandments. All the other nine are moral laws, not ceremonial or judicial. This Decalogue is constantly appealed to by the New Testament when it speaks of righteousness. Sabbath-keeping is included in the Bible's most eminent code of morality.

Jesus Christ, by his teaching, deepens our under-standing of the spiritual nature of the fourth command-ment. He instructed on that subject often. In his teachings he pledged that he would take up direction of the weekly Sabbath as a feature of his kingdom. His reign as Lord would give significant attention to the Sabbath. Those who were most intimate with Jesus (the apostles) began to worship on the first day of the week instead of on the seventh, and the church has done so ever since.

All of this is plain and obvious. Yet, perhaps you are not satisfied. You want a more clear explanation of why the day was changed. There is one, but it will take careful study to comprehend it. The Bible explanation cannot stand all by itself without the above Biblical information. Nor will this Bible passage shine with bright transparency that will immediately convince all who read it. But we are addressing a very small point of truth. We are answering only the questions: 1. For what reason has the Sabbath Day been changed from the seventh to the first day of the week? 2. Is such a change fully consistent with the continuing validity of the moral law? 3. Does this change of day undermine the fourth commandment?

Sometimes children are very unreasonable. It is possible for them impatiently to demand an answer to any question they ask. When told that the solution contains things not easily understood, they may further demand that a simple explanation be given. Some need to realize what Hebrews 5:11 tells us, 'We have much to say about this, but it is hard to explain because you are slow to learn.' When Christians' minds ought to be used to theological and Biblical patterns of thought, they may yet be like very small children who cannot eat meat. They still need to be fed milk and baby food. These 'babes' often cry the most insistently that the loftiest truths be put into their nursing bottles of proof-text theology. But we have to work hard to understand some things. One must mature through an habitual pattern of exercising his mind before he can even begin to work through some truths.

Yes, the New Testament gives an answer regarding the change of the Sabbath Day from the seventh to the first. It is found in the book of Hebrews. You might have expected that. This is the book written to Jewish believers who faced a struggle that the Gentiles never experienced. They had served the Lord under the Mosaic covenant. Now they served Messiah under the

New Covenant. Some had memories of spiritual blessings before Messiah came. They had loved the temple, the priesthood, the sacrifices, the traditions of Judaism because their hearts had worshipped God and he had spoken to them in these institutions. Now everything was changing. God, in judgment, was about to dismantle their beloved and familiar system of life, worship and service. Yes, they had the church of Christ which would remain. But it had been so comfortable to have some years to live in both the Jewish and the Christian ways of worship. Now the temple, the priesthood, the Jewish arrangement as they knew it would be destroyed with Jerusalem in 70 AD.

Much of the book of Hebrews is teaching how the Christian religion has replaced the Jewish covenant. It explains how the New Covenant in Christ fulfills and surpasses in glory everything the spiritual Jews had loved. Often the writer is poised to go on, but he realizes that the minds of his readers are not trained to take in any more. Indeed, they may be missing much that he has already said.

In addition to the comfort given these discouraged Jewish Christians, the Book of Hebrews recognizes that they are in peculiar danger of turning their backs on Christ out of preference for the older Mosaic covenant. Hence the book is filled with strong and lengthy exhortations that they persevere in their faith in Christ Jesus.

You will get a taste for the complexity of this Book of Hebrews and the concentration needed to read it by looking at Hebrews chapters 3 and 4. At the end of chapter 2 the writer had introduced the idea that Jesus Christ is the supreme high priest. However, the thought is not really developed until the end of chapter

4. Between 2:18 and 4:14, both of which develop the priesthood of Christ, we have a lengthy exhortation to persevere (*3:1–4:13*). This is not unusual for Hebrews. There is another lengthy interruption of the subject (*5:11–6:20*) for rebuke and exhortation before its thoughts on the priesthood of Christ are fully worked out.

Hebrews begins to exhort believers to have confidence in Jesus the high priest (*3:1*) only to encourage that confidence by showing how much greater Christ is than was Moses (*3:2–6*). At this point the exhortation becomes a warning to the Hebrew Christians not to fail to receive everlasting blessings through unbelief. The writer does this by a lengthy exposition of Psalm 95:7–11 which he quotes in full in 3:7–11. It is in this section, subordinate to his discussion of Jesus Christ being the great high priest, and subordinate to a lesser point, namely, that Christ is far superior to Moses, that the issue of the Sabbath arises. Sabbath is enfolded in many layers of other issues being discussed. Only careful thought can follow the arguments.

An apostolic choice of Psalm 95:7–11 for this exhortation is most interesting. Psalm 95 breaks the pattern of the Book of Psalms. Most often, if there is a negative note, it comes at the start of a psalm. The psalmist is discouraged about something and expresses his heaviness of heart. Yet, as he prays his attitude becomes more and more cheerful and hopeful near the end of the psalm. Psalm 95 begins with bright and happy praise only to end with a stunning curse.

It is even more astounding to note how the writer interprets the awesome and terrifying close of Psalm 95. God swears in his anger, 'They shall never enter my rest.' Those are the closing words of Psalm 95. This apostle finds in those words a promise that some *must* enter rest (*4:1* and *6*)! He finds in this withering curse – a promise! And he uses that promise as the basis of encouraging the Hebrew Christians not to fall short of the promise (*4:1*) as their ancestors had fallen short of Canaan in the desert (*3:16–19*). Stern warning in Psalm 95 contains a kernel of hope. We are hastening over so much important material to try to get to the point of our little book on the Sabbath. Yet certain elements in this exhortation of Hebrews 3 and 4 cannot be ignored. One such feature is the prominent discussion of the word 'rest'.

This word is first introduced by the quotation of Psalm 95:11. 'They shall never enter my rest' (*Hebrews 3:11*). Of course, in the psalm this was spoken of the disobedient Hebrews in Moses' day who failed to enter Canaan. Their example was used by the prophet David to urge the people of his day, 'Today, if you hear his voice, do not harden your hearts.' The writer to the Hebrews discovers our present day gospel in the words of this 95th Psalm, especially as it relates to the idea of rest.

Hebrews works out the comparison in this way: We have had the gospel preached to us just as did the ancient Jews in the desert (*4:2*). We who have believed the gospel are entering into rest (*4:3*). Those who heard the gospel in God's voice in the desert did not have faith (*3:19* and *4:2*). This lack of faith is evidenced in their disobedience or sin (*3:16–18*). Christians then are urged not to harden their hearts with sin but to hold fast their confidence in Christ lest they too come short of the promise of rest (*3:12–14*). Only as we persevere can we say that we have become sharers in Christ (*3:14*). The Jews in the desert came short of the promised rest. We Christians must endure to the end in faith and righteousness and thus fully enter the rest.

It is important to notice something about which the author of Hebrews is very careful. To this point it has not been mentioned in our survey. The rest into which men are called to enter is specifically God's rest! 'They shall never enter *my* rest' (*Psalm 95:11* and *Hebrews 3:11*). Thus, 3:18 speaks of entering '*his* rest', 4:1 'entering *his* rest', 4:3 'enter *that* rest' and 'enter *my* rest'. Again, 4:5 says 'enter *my* rest'. 4:6 does not use the word 'rest' as inserted in the NIV. The final exhortation in 4:11 is that we must make every effort to enter '*that* rest'. In the preponderance of cases the apostle insists that the gospel has to do with entering God's rest. The rest (one and only) is God's rest. It is not achieving their own rest but entering his.

It is this noted feature of the promise in Psalm 95 which leads the apostle to his comments in 4:3b and 4: 'And yet the works were finished since the creation of the world. For somewhere he has spoken about the seventh day in these words: "And on the seventh day God rested from all his works."' If those who believe the present-day gospel are entering God's rest as 4:3a claims, then it is important to identify what the rest of God is. This the writer does in verses 3b and 4.

On the seventh day of creation, God entered his rest. All his works were finished. All the display of God's glory in his works was completed. Therefore, the Almighty ceased working on the seventh day. Again, the chief issue is not non-activity on God's part but full enjoyment of his work and the receiving of glory from the work of his hands. However, he did not intend to enter this rest alone. From the seventh day of creation, man has been called into God's rest. Man is to share with God the pleasure and satisfaction of all God's work. Man is to glorify God, not for some future personal blessing but for God's finished work. Man is to be God's special companion in the enjoyment of God's finished work and in giving God glory for his finished work.

Again we must note in passing how unbiblical is the notion that Sabbath rest for man was initiated only at the time of the Exodus. God's rest from his finished work has called to man to enter his rest since the seventh day of creation. The truly astounding thing which the author tells us in Hebrews 4:3 is that we who believe the gospel are entering God's rest which existed from the creation week.

But as soon as the writer of Hebrews notes the existence of God's rest from creation and the call to men to enter God's rest with him, he reminds us of the words, 'They shall never enter my rest.' In other words, God's rest was complete from the beginning of the world. Man was called to enter that rest with God from the seventh day of creation. Yet because of sin, rebellion, hardness of heart, and unbelief, men did not enter in. Men have come short of God's rest because of the Fall.

Still, Hebrews is not finished with this idea of God's rest and men entering into it. Verse 6 tells us that in spite of human rebellion and failure to enter God's rest (as illustrated in the perishing of the Jews in the desert) it still remains that some men will enter the rest of God. 'Therefore' (*verse 7*) in David's day God calls again to men, 'Today if you hear his voice, do not harden your hearts.' God has not given up on his purpose that men should enter his rest.

Realizing what the Jews might think of this turn in

his thoughts the writer quickly adds verse 8. The Jewish Christians might think, 'Of course God persisted in calling men to rest. After some Jews perished in the wilderness due to unbelief and disobedience, Joshua led other Jews into the rest of Canaan.' 'Aha!,' they would think, 'true Jews in the land really entered God's rest.'

'No!' says the writer of Hebrews. 'If Joshua had given them rest' and thus fulfilled the promise that some must enter God's rest, then God would not later, in the days of David, have spoken of another day. It was David, long after Joshua, who urged, '*Today* . . . harden not your hearts.' God's rest was not entered into by following Joshua into Canaan. But we who believe the gospel of Jesus Christ 'are entering into the rest' of God (*4:3*). It is only faith in Jesus Christ that leads fallen men of the Old Testament or the New into God's rest.

The reason for this is clear. Never was there anything lacking in God's rest. His works were finished from creation week. He entered his perfect rest. And from the time of the seventh day he has called men to enter into his rest with him. What was lacking was in man. Fallen man was hard of heart, disobedient to the promise of God and rebellious at the call of God to enter his rest. Our gospel of Jesus Christ provides what is lacking in man to enable him to enter God's perfect rest. In Christ, the invitation to enter God's rest comes to us *today*.

All of this is the context preparing us for verses 9 and 10 and the specific statement about the Christian Sabbath. 'There remains, then, a keeping of a Sabbath for the people of God; for he who did enter his rest did rest from all his works, even as God did from his.'

English translations of these words are quite diverse and often misleading. Translators have felt that it was necessary to clarify what the apostle meant by altering exactly what he said. This is certainly understandable from the complexity of the context.

For the first time in his discussion of rest the apostle mentions a Sabbath Day. There remains then 'a keeping of a Sabbath', or 'a Sabbath observance' for the people of God. It is unfortunate that the King James translated this word of verse 9 'rest'. Twelve times the word 'rest' is used from 3:11 to 4:11. Always the author's word for 'rest' is a totally different one from the word used in verse 9. The NIV has no textual reason to translate it 'Sabbath rest' for the word 'rest', used 12 times, is not repeated in verse 9. This word refers obviously to a Sabbath-keeping or Sabbath observance or a Sabbath Day to be kept by the people of God. There is a New Covenant Sabbath Day!

Verse 10 gives an explanation of this. 'For he who did enter his rest did rest from all his works, even as God did from his.' Only a pronoun is used to refer to someone who entered his own rest. In entering his own rest, this person rested from all his works just as God on the seventh day of creation rested from all of his. Furthermore, his finished act of entering his own rest is the explanation for all the people of God keeping a Sabbath in the New Covenant.

Some, like the NIV translators, suggest that the pronoun 'he' is indefinite, referring to every Christian, every believer. This cannot be for two reasons. Never in the context does the author refer to a believer entering his own rest. It is always God's rest he enters. Never does a man cease from his own works with satisfaction in them. He enters God's rest to glorify him for *his* works. Furthermore, the 'he' referred to has *once for all* finished *his* works (aorist tense). He has *once for all* entered his rest (aorist tense). It is past and finished for him as God's works were completed on the seventh day. Hebrews 4:3 speaks of believers as those who *are entering God's* rest but not as *having entered* their *own* rest. They are yet in process of entering the works of Another! And this person's activity ('he who did enter his rest') is the reason why all of God's people in the New Covenant still have a Sabbath observance.

Now, momentarily, it may seem plausible to say that the future-hoped-for-rest of every Christian, which does not yet exist, is the reason for a Christian Sabbath. However, such a thought does not at all fit with the passage. It does not agree with the context in its general thought or in its specific wording. A future tense is not used.

It is still God's perfect rest, complete from the time of creation, that we who believe are entering. Nothing has been lacking in the promised rest. However, much of hardness of heart, unbelief, disobedience and rebellion in fallen human beings have made men fall short of God's rest. To remedy man's sin Christ came. And 'today' the gospel calls sinners to enter God's rest through the Messiah (*3:15*).

It is *Christ* who has once for all entered his rest when he rose victorious from the grave. It is *Christ* who once for all has ceased from his own works of redemption as God did from his of creation. Christ's ceasing from his works occurred on the first day of the week, just as God's ceasing from his was on the seventh day. Christ, the mediator of the New Covenant, has become Lord of the Sabbath. Sabbath-keeping is under his reign and is a definite part of the activity of those who are in his kingdom. His finished work enables men to enter God's creation rest. Hence, Sabbath-keeping in the New Covenant is on the first day of the week and not on the seventh.

There is only one serious objection to the above understanding of verses 9 and 10. That objection is the use of a pronoun to refer to Christ when the antecedent to the pronoun is not near at hand. However, there are a number of very plausible answers to this objection. Exactly the same thing is done in Hebrews 4:13. Reference is made to Christ by using a pronoun when his name is not found in the immediately preceding context.

Furthermore, the entire theme of the book is the superiority of Christ to Mosaic institutions. The major theme of this passage is Jesus Christ, our great high priest. This particular exhortation began with the exaltation of Jesus Christ as far superior to Moses. In the midst of this exhortation we are urged to be sharers in Christ or partakers of Christ (*3:14*). The entire argumentation is that we who believe (in Christ and his gospel) are entering into God's rest. He is the way for sinners to enter God's rest. Joshua did not lead anyone into that rest. Only Christ can do so.

It is perfectly natural, then, for our minds to turn to Christ in Hebrews 4:9 and 10 when these verses speak of someone who has (once for all) entered his rest and ceased from his works as God did from his. It is compelling that we think only of Christ when this finished work of an individual becomes the focal point of New Covenant Sabbath observance. The New Covenant has not turned us in upon ourselves as the reason for Sabbath-keeping. It points to the finished work of Christ which admits sinners to the finished work of the Father.

By understanding Hebrews 3 and 4, the Christian will have little difficulty in following the apostles and the church of all ages in worshipping on the first day of the week instead of the seventh. Questions as to the reasons for the change will fall away. It will be obvious that in Christ the fourth commandment reaches its highest glory. A change of day honours the creation rest of God and in no way injures the Sabbath law.

However, if you are looking for a text of one sentence which you can read and thereby silence all Seventh Day Adventists, antinomians and anti-Sabbatarians, you will be disappointed. Those who want a 'quickie' answer will not sit still long enough to study Hebrews 3 and 4 with you. Immature saints will not be able to follow the reasoning of the apostle. Their minds are not trained by use to grapple with Scripture. Those who bring prejudices to Hebrews 4:9 and 10 will 'see' other things.

May all humble, seeking Bible students gain understanding from these verses! May your conscience be set at rest regarding the New Testament's continued adherence to the fourth commandment, but the change of the actual day of the week on which we worship. A seventh day Sabbath under the Old Testament marked the promise and privilege of mankind entering God's rest with him. A first day Sabbath under the New Testament marks the promise and privilege of mankind entering God's rest with him and the possibility of doing so as a sinner through the finished redemptive work of Jesus Christ.

8

DIFFICULT CASES OF CONSCIENCE

And this is my prayer: that your love may abound more and more in knowledge and depth of insight, so that you may be able to discern what is best and may be pure and blameless until the day of Christ, filled with the fruit of righteousness that comes through Jesus Christ – to the glory and praise of God.

[Philippians 1:9–11]

Christians will be plagued with doubts and questions about the Sabbath long after this book has been written. Nevertheless, certain leading sources of confusion which persist must here be addressed in order to give sincere students of God's Word some hints for grappling with their difficulties.

I. TEXTS WHICH SEEM TO DENY THAT THERE IS A CHRISTIAN SABBATH

No doubt as you have read through Paul's letters to the Gentile churches you have noted three passages which, on the surface, appear to have reference to the fourth commandment. All three deny in rather strong language that Christians have any obligation to keep certain days holy.

The first such statement is to be found in the midst of Paul's thorough discussion of a Christian's use of things indifferent. 'One man considers one day more sacred than another; another man considers every day alike. Each one should be fully convinced in his own mind. He who regards one day as special, does so to the Lord . . . and he who abstains, does so to the Lord . . .' (*Romans 14:5–6*).

The remaining two instances occur in sections of Paul's letters which are concerned to show that it is no longer appropriate for Christians to be bound to certain Old Testament regulations. These two are far more negative in tone regarding the observance of days. 'How is it that you are turning back to those weak and miserable principles? Do you wish to be enslaved by them all over again? You are observing special days and months and seasons and years! I fear for you, that somehow I have wasted my efforts on you' (*Galatians 4:9–11*). The most striking and troublesome is the last. 'Therefore do not let anyone judge you by what you eat or drink, or with regard to a religious festival, a New Moon celebration or a Sabbath day. These are a shadow of the things that were to come; the reality, however, is found in Christ' (*Colossians 2:16–17*).

At first glance these verses seem to support those who argue that there is no sacred day whatever in the New Testament. Romans 14 indicates that making a day holy (whichever day it refers to) is a matter of personal preference. A man may or may not make certain days special as he wishes. Galatians 4 becomes more stern. There, believers are rebuked for returning to Old Testament patterns of worship, like observing days (whichever day it refers to). Paul is unhappy that they are returning to former slavery! Colossians 2 remarks that a Sabbath day (whichever it refers to) was an Old Testament shadow. Since we have the reality foreshadowed, that is, Christ, we no longer have need for the shadow.

Do these texts refer to the weekly Sabbath Days required in the Ten Commandments?

To begin to answer, let us recall that Jesus our Lord plainly announced that he would personally assume authority over the weekly Sabbath, including within his own kingdom this institution which is so beneficial to all mankind (*Mark 2:27 & 28*). In Hebrews we saw that there does remain a Sabbath observance for God's people in the gospel age (*Hebrews 4:9*). Why then would the above three texts wear the appearance of contradicting other New Testament Scriptures? A satisfying answer may be found only in a wider study of the Biblical doctrine of the law. Our conclusions must be supportive of all that the New Testament teaches on this subject. There are certainly no true contradictions in God's holy Word.

It does appear that Romans 14, Galatians 4 and Colossians 2 are all speaking of the same kind of days – days of Jewish worship which the Christian is no longer obligated to observe. At Rome there was an obvious diversity of practice, some keeping the days holy, some not doing so. Paul only instructed them not to be critical of those whose practice differed from their own. A Christian *could* keep these Jewish days, but he did not *have* to do so.

At Galatia certain leaders had begun to teach that Christians *must* be circumcised and required to obey the law of Moses, including the observance of these days. In this book Paul emphasized the judicial nature of such regulations regarding days. They were restrictive and binding, like slavery itself. No Christian should desire to return to slavery.

At Colosse Paul was stressing the ceremonial nature of these institutions regarding days. He tells us that they were appointed in the Mosaic covenant to depict great truths about the coming Messiah. Dim images of Christ were set before the Jews in these observances. However, once Christ came in person and we have received the full revelation of his person and work it is quite appropriate for the believer to lay aside the shadows of Christ. Instead we should look full in his wonderful face.

It is apparent that these three texts are describing ceremonial and judicial laws of Moses. Their observance was required of the Jews but they had no authority over the Christian. A Jewish believer may choose to continue his participation in these ceremonies of worship but he may not demand that others do so. Again we ask the all-important question – Is the weekly Sabbath such a ceremonial and judicial law?

As we have noted before, the weekly Sabbath law is to be found in the midst of the Ten Commandments. Everything else about that code of law is entirely moral, nothing else being of a judicial or ceremonial nature. This summary of moral righteousness is in the New Testament (*Matthew 5:17–48, Romans 13:8–10, James 2:10–11*, to mention but a few such places) upheld as the Christian standard of morality. Jesus frequently underscored the importance of understanding the fourth commandment in particular. Moral law is not suspended in the New Covenant as were judicial and ceremonial laws.

Weekly Sabbath-keeping as required in the fourth commandment does not fit the description of days described in Romans 14, Galatians 4 and Colossians 2. It was *not* instituted in the time of Moses when other temporary ceremonies were introduced. The weekly Sabbath day is a creation ordinance just as is marriage.

Moses said so (*Genesis 2:1–3*)! Jesus said so (*Mark 2:27, 28*)! So did the author of Hebrews 4:3–4!

The Decalogue's fourth commandment does not point forward to Christ with shadowy images of him. It clearly points back to creation and to God's rest. Even when our Lord Jesus changed its observance from the seventh day to the first because it was then that he had finished his redemptive work, still the emphatic concern is that man enter God's rest, which has been fully enjoyed from the creation of the world. We who believe in Christ are entering God's rest which he entered on the seventh day of creation. The weekly Sabbath is *not* a ceremonial law. Isaiah showed us that it was *not* a burdensome, enslaving judicial law. So did our Lord Jesus!

To what days, then, are Romans 14, Galatians 4 and Colossians 2 referring? Is there another possibility beside the weekly Sabbath of the fourth commandment? In addition to the weekly Sabbath required in the Ten Commandments, each year the Jews under Moses observed a number of other Sabbath days. You may read of most of them in Leviticus 23. They were very sacred days observed in connection with Passover, Firstfruits (Pentecost), Feast of Weeks, Feast of Trumpets, Day of Atonement, and Feast of Tabernacles. All of these are filled with imagery of Christ's person and work. They are shadows. There are elaborate, detailed requirements (judicial regulations) surrounding these Sabbath days. It is these Sabbaths which naturally come to mind in connection with 'months and seasons and years' in Galatians 4 and with 'religious festivals and New Moon celebrations' in Colossians 2. It is only an attempt to refer these 'days' and 'Sabbath day' to the weekly Sabbath which brings conflict and contradiction between Scriptures.

2. BUT DIDN'T THE CONTINENTAL REFORMERS OMIT THE FOURTH COMMANDMENT?

It would be most difficult to build any doctrine through a survey of history alone. There are many strands of evidence among which every historian must be selective. And yet we have such a high regard for the wisdom and leadership of the Protestant Reformers. The Spirit of our God was upon them and they taught the Scriptures with remarkable integrity.

To be fair, it must be noted that neither John Calvin nor some of the other Reformers held to the view of the Westminster Confession of Faith on the Sabbath. It must also be mentioned, however, that they did often insist upon a day for Christian worship. Even today the wisest ministers, among those who believe that the Lord's day has nothing to do with the fourth commandment, recognize the necessity of an entire day for worship if Christians and the church are to be spiritually healthy. It is an interesting endorsement on the practical level for the Sabbath law.

Some of the Continental Reformers and Reformation creeds reason something like this. Christians have ceased from seeking God's favour by good works and have instead relied upon the works of Jesus Christ to save them. This rest of the Christian from a works way of salvation is akin to God's ceasing from his works at creation. The Old Testament weekly Sabbath prefigured this resting upon Christ. Now we have the reality and no longer need the shadow. However, Christians, too, need a day of worship; but the Lord's Day is not identical with the fourth commandment Sabbath.

At best this is a jumble of poorly worked-through ideas. At worst some of the Reformers have misled us at this point. It appears that some Reformed thinkers could not escape the influence of one of their leading doctrines even when it did not apply to the subject which they were handling.

Some who are newly come to the doctrines of grace find God's sovereignty in every Bible verse and feel compelled to expound that theme in every message. A few Reformers seemed to feel compelled to discuss justification by faith when defining the nature of Sabbath-keeping. To them ceasing from works could only mean to cease to rely on works religion to be saved. However, the parallel does not hold in Biblical passages on the subject.

God ceased from glorious and righteous works when he entered his rest. He entered rest satisfied and delighted in the work he had done. When the Jews were called to work six days and rest on the seventh in imitation of their Creator, it was not being suggested that they try to earn salvation by their obedience to the law. Such a course was nowhere recommended by Moses! Galatians 3 explicitly denies such a position. All mankind was given six days to do all his own legitimate works. On the seventh he was to cease from these (good) works to worship and serve the Lord. Man is to share God's delight in divine works. He is to enter God's rest, which has nothing to do with a former miserable works religion.

Our Lord Jesus found the practice of the fourth commandment consistent with the principles and aims of his kingdom. As Hebrews teaches us, all of the works that are finished which hold the attention of Sabbath observers are good works of the Father and the Son.

It is time to turn our attention to another category of questions regarding the Sabbath day. There is a great variety of assaults against the validity of the fourth commandment as a Christian moral law. However much it may perplex the Christian to answer these attacks, he has not crossed all of the difficult hurdles when he has put to silence anti-Sabbatarians and his own uncertainties in this matter. There is a host of difficult decisions to be made in practical application of the principles for Sabbath observance.

3. WHAT IS PROPER SABBATH BEHAVIOUR?

When some Christians come to believe that it is their duty to keep the Sabbath Day holy, they become very fearful lest they engage in the wrong activities on the Lord's Day. Such apprehension often takes the form of wanting very specific answers from a minister or a counsellor. May I go bicycle-riding on Sunday? Is it all right to go jogging on the Lord's Day? Should I purchase medicine for a child with a sore throat? It is as if the believer is collecting a large list of items, next to which he is writing 'do' or 'don't'.

This sort of inquiry regarding explicit details of behaviour is, unfortunately, encouraged by a type of church leader who feeds his ego by promoting himself as a kind of ethical guru. Wishing to be the ideal elder or conscientious teacher this 'leader' offers direction in minute particulars of living. His style of handling practical issues of living makes his people utterly dependent upon his counsel. His people become incapable of coping with decisions unless the 'oracle of wisdom' has decreed exact permission or prohibition. Momentarily, it may seem wonderfully good fortune to have such an involved counsellor giving precise directives, but in the end it makes dependent children of those who ask.

At the head of this chapter is printed Paul's prayer for the Philippians. He asked the Lord to increase his flock's knowledge and depth of insight. These gifts he desired for them so that *they* would be able to discern what is best when confronted with any decision. It was never intended that God's people be given exhaustively itemized delineation of what to do in every circumstance. He did not place elders in leadership so that they might dictate what specific course to follow in every particular. He does not give divine revelation as to which alternative to choose at a given moment.

Our Lord has given us the great principles of his Word. Also, he has sent the Holy Spirit to assist our understanding, so that, in any given set of alternatives requiring judgment, the individual saint will be exercised in spirit. Only by inner wrestlings will he increase in discernment of what is best. In Hebrews 5:14 we are told that 'solid food is for the mature, who by constant use have trained *themselves* to distinguish good from evil'. It may seem comfortable to have a list to tick off without thought. However, the truth is that such practice atrophies the mind and heart.

General principles from God's Word are adequate guidelines to equip a Christian, aided by the Holy Spirit, to face every eventuality. The Sabbath Day is to be kept in mind. It is to be devoted with joy to the worship and service of God. This day is special and is not to be cluttered with our work or with the employment of others, except so far as will serve in God's worship, in man's necessities, and in showing mercy to our fellow human beings. God's Word is a sufficient guide. All that is needed is for the individual Christian to exercise his personal discernment as to what is best. Thus he trains himself to distinguish good from evil.

Included in this exercise is the necessity of becoming independent of others. The fear of man's opinion regarding your application of these principles must not keep you from applying the principles before God. This is a freedom of conscience given us in Jesus Christ. It must not be surrendered to anyone. Being subject to our Lord and his Word demands that we keep ourselves free from the tyranny of human opinion, even 'expert' opinion.

Many of the particular questions men and women ask cannot be given a definite answer. More rests upon motive and intent than upon the outward acts we do on the Sabbath. 'May I go bicycle-riding on Sunday?' Because younger children are not equipped to discern their own heart motives or the application of general principles, parents must make some rules for their households. Perhaps one family will have children who are so attached to bicycle-riding on six days of the week, that they will tell their children, 'No bicycle-riding on Sunday.' They intend to make the day special by filling it with different activity on the Lord's Day.

As soon as one parent tells his child, 'We do not ride bicycles on Sunday; it is the Lord's Day,' along will come a Christian neighbour with his children – all riding bicycles! His motive may have been to give his young children necessary exercise so that they can be still at evening worship. This family is riding together to the park where they will find a quiet spot to work on Scripture memory.

'Is it all right to go jogging on the Lord's Day?' Some Christians are fitness fanatics. They jog for seven miles every day, increasing their endurance, checking heart rate, etc. To them it is an all-consuming exercise. They do well to decide to devote the day to the Lord and not to take from him a major portion of his holy time. For them jogging would distract from joyful communion with God.

A Christian friend may very much be motivated by a desire to spend Sunday afternoon in reading Biblical books or in prayer. However, he has a job which requires him to sit at a desk all week long. As he attempts his Sunday afternoon reading, he may nod off to sleep and have no devotions. Next time, he will run a half mile to get his blood moving so that more time can be given to spiritual communion with God when he finishes.

In these and hundreds of instances like them, the thing which matters is whether the heart is crying, 'Thy face will I seek, O Lord.' Small children and elderly folk cannot give the same degree of concentration and energy to the Lord in a single day that young adults can endure and it should not be expected. Legalistic and Pharisaic minds will imagine that if they cannot jog and still keep the Sabbath holy, then neither can any of their brothers. This is just the way man-made rules begin to be made and oppressive traditions start.

In the end, a heavy-handed legalism will do more to drive people away from Sabbath observance than it will do to preserve the day. Our weekly Sabbaths are intended to be joyful in the Lord and good for us, body and soul.

There are very complex questions regarding the Sabbath and society at large. Ignorance of our God and his truth is profound in our Western world. There are multitudes of whom it may be said that God is not in any of their thoughts. How does a Christian individual or a church begin to address the Sabbath issue in our wider society? To what extent can principles regarding Sabbath observance be applied to a heathen nation now that Mosaic systems are inappropriate for the Christian and for the unbeliever? How much must a Christian suffer at the hands of a godless economic system in order to worship and serve the Lord?

No easy solutions come to mind for these important puzzles. Yet may it not be hoped that, as individual Christians abound more and more in depth of insight, and as they serve as salt in society, some answers may begin to be given to our wider questions? To attain such Spirit-filled expertise we must all be in training week by week to distinguish good from evil with regard to this fourth commandment.

Through the widespread decline of public worship of any kind, our nations have become more and more oriented to material things. Because so many never give a day to the contemplation of heavenly and spiritual realities, their shoulders are bent over and their eyes are riveted upon the clay of this earth. But man has a soul, however neglected and overlooked. Spiritual aspects of human nature are crying out for attention and satisfaction. There is more to life than food and drink, than gold, silver, clothing and entertainment. A man's life does not consist in the abundance of things which he possesses. It is urgent that men realize this.

Although sceptics sneer at the fourth commandment, it is nevertheless true that the benefits of the Sabbath Day call out unto the deeps within man. A day each week to commune with God! A day to become acquainted with the true and living God, to hear of his truth and grace. Sadly, while many Christians are abandoning God's call to attend holy assemblies with himself, spiritually starved materialists, who cannot live with their meaningless 'freedom' from the law, are turning to cults and to Eastern mysticism.

The modern man or the modern woman, at sea in an ocean of materialism without a spiritual compass, will not be reached merely by individual approaches. Rather, the reaching out must come from congregations where there are weekly holy days of spiritual assembly, spiritual worship, spiritual fellowship and spiritual service. Where people have learned in joyful exuberance to worship the Lord and keep his day holy, a powerful attraction will attend their witness.

No age has ever more intensely needed Sabbath-keeping than ours. Attempts to scrap God's moral law and to replace it with institutions and schemes of human invention are miserably failing. Sabbath-keeping in isolation is not an answer to all man's ills. Yet, this law is intimately related to all others and has a necessary connection with the other branches of God's moral code. Where even small segments of mankind have succeeded in implementing a joyful observance of the Sabbath, they have reaped enormous benefit. It is time for us, too, to call the Sabbath a delight and to return unto the Lord.

List of Outstanding Materials on the Sabbath

This study has not been written because no good works on the subject of the Sabbath are in print. On the contrary there is an abundance of learned and forceful material available, much of it reprinted from ages past.

It is the calling of every generation to contend for the faith which was once for all entrusted to the saints (*Jude 3*). Ours it is to stand upon the shoulders of apostles, prophets and other giants to repeat what they have taught us from God's Word. It is not our task to invent or discover new things. Yet our present day church will need fresh exposition of old truths addressing their peculiar questions and circumstances. Far more satisfaction is to be found in recounting ancient but eternal verities than may be experienced in hearing and telling of new things.

Many resources are available to assist your study of this great Sabbath theme. A few of them are here suggested to you:

Roger Beckwith and Wilfred Stott – *The Christian Sunday*, 1978, Baker Book House, Grand Rapids, Michigan (1, 2).

John Brown – *An Exposition of The Epistle To The Galatians*, 1853, Edinburgh. Commentary on chapter 3, while not on the Sabbath deals with the law under Moses and the law under Christ.

Robert Dabney – 'The Christian Sabbath: Its Nature, Design and Proper Observance' in *Discussions Evangelical and Theological* vol. 1, 1967, Banner of Truth Trust, London.

James T. Dennison, Jr. – *The Market Day of the Soul*, 1983, University Press of America, Lanham, Maryland (1, 2).

Jonathan Edwards – 'The Perpetuity and Change of the Sabbath' (three sermons) in *The Works of Jonathan Edwards* vol. 2, pp. 93–103, 1974, Banner of Truth Trust, Edinburgh.

Patrick Fairbairn – *The Revelation of Law in Scripture*, 1957, Zondervan, Grand Rapids, Michigan.

Matthew Henry – 'A Serious Address to those that profane the Lord's Day' in vol. 1 of *The Complete Works of the Rev. Matthew Henry*, 1979, Baker Book House, Grand Rapids, Michigan.

Archibald A. Hodge – 'The Day Changed and The Sabbath Preserved', Committee on Christian Education, The Orthodox Presbyterian Church, Philadelphia, Pennsylvania.

Erroll Hulse – 'Sanctifying the Lord's Day: Reformed and Puritan Attitudes' in *Aspects of Sanctification* (Westminster Conference of 1981), Evangelical Press, Hertfordshire (1, 2).

John Murray – 'The Sabbath Institution' (1); 'The Pattern of the Lord's Day'; 'The Relevance of the Sabbath' in *Collected Writings* vol. 1, 1976, Banner of Truth Trust, Edinburgh.

John Murray – 'Creation Ordinances' in *Principles of Conduct*, 1957, Eerdmans, Grand Rapids, Michigan.

John Owen – *An Exposition of the Epistle To The Hebrews*, 1812, Edinburgh, Exercitations 35–40; Commentary on Hebrews chapters 3 and 4.

James I. Packer – 'The Puritans and the Lord's Day', Puritan Conference Papers for 1957, 1958, London (1, 2).

Philip Schaff – *History of the Christian Church*, vol. 1
Apostolic Christianity pp. 476–480, 1950, Eerdmans, Grand Rapids, Michigan (2).

Benjamin B. Warfield – 'The Foundations of the
Sabbath in the Word of God' in *Selected Shorter
Writings of Benjamin B. Warfield – I*, 1970, Presby-
terian and Reformed, Nutley, New Jersey.

Daniel Wilson – *The Divine Authority and Perpetual
Obligation of the Lord's Day*, 1956, Lord's Day
Observance Society, London.

Westminster Confession of Faith – Chapter XXI.
Westminster Larger Catechism – Questions 115–121.
Westminster Shorter Catechism – Questions 57–62.

(1) Additional Bibliography available in these works.
(2) Extensive historic material included in these works.

SOME OTHER
BANNER OF TRUTH
TITLES

SIGNS OF THE APOSTLES
Walter Chantry

How should the Christian assess contemporary claims about spiritual gifts? Walter Chantry believes that God is still working in the world today. But it is his conviction that miraculous powers are no longer placed in the hands of individual men and women.

Tracing the occurrence of miracles in the Old and New Testaments, he concludes that their function was primarily to attest the commission of the spokesman of God. This is why, he maintains, every recorded instance of the reception of miraculous power in the New Testament Church occurred through the ministry of an Apostle. Now that the canon of Scripture is complete, Walter Chantry believes that the pursuit of all the spiritual gifts of the apostolic age can only proceed upon the basis of a failure to recognize the sufficiency and finality of the Bible.

Walter Chantry was born in 1938 at Norristown, Pennsylvania, raised in the Presbyterian Church; graduated B.A. in History from Dickinson College, Carlisle in 1960, and B.D. from Westminster Theological Seminary in 1963, from which time he has been pastor of Grace Baptist Church, Carlisle.

ISBN 0 85151 175 9
160pp., paperback

GOD'S RIGHTEOUS KINGDOM
The Law's Connection with the Gospel
Walter Chantry

The Gospel is always open to two abuses – legalism, on the one hand, which destroys the saving grace of God, and antinomianism on the other, which sets grace against the responsibility of obedience in the Christian.

In the space of twelve chapters, Walter Chantry expounds the relationship of the Law to the Gospel in a way which touches contemporary controversy; but he does so through painstaking exposition of the Scriptures, so that his message has abiding relevance. In particular he deals with the kind of question which troubles many ordinary Christians – Were there two ways of salvation in the Old and New Testaments? Do the Old Testament laws all apply in the same way today, or do they apply to us at all? What was Jesus' attitude to the Law? How does the Sabbath day fit in?

Short chapters, clearly argued, written in a popular style and with practical applications always in mind, this is a book with an important message for contemporary Christians.

ISBN 0 85151 310 7
154pp., paperback

TODAY'S GOSPEL
Authentic or Synthetic?
Walter Chantry

In this arousing work Walter Chantry expounds from Christ's dealing with the Rich Young Ruler the essential elements in Gospel preaching. A close examination of the Scripture evidence leads to this conclusion:

'Differences between much of today's preaching and that of Jesus are not petty; they are enormous. The chief errors are not in emphasis or approach but in the heart of the Gospel message. Were there a deficiency in one of the areas mentioned in these pages, it would be serious. But to ignore all – the attributes of God, the holy law of God, repentance, a call to bow to the enthroned Christ – and to pervert the doctrine of assurance, is the most vital mistake.

'Incredulity may grip you. Can so many evangelicals be so wrong? . . . All are not in error, but great hosts are. All have not perverted the gospel to the same degree, but many are terribly far from the truth. All those who "make decisions" are not deceived, but great numbers are. Above all, few *care* to recover the Gospel message . . .'.

This powerfully-written book has a message which goes to the heart of the contemporary problem in a way that conferences and commissions on evangelism have failed to do. Its expository approach is particularly valuable.

ISBN 0 85151 027 2
96pp., paperback

THE SHADOW OF THE CROSS
Studies in Self-Denial
Walter Chantry

The message of the Cross is the heart of the Christian gospel. The records of the life of Jesus devote more attention to it than any other part of his ministry. The rest of the New Testament constantly underlines its centrality for Christian faith.

But Jesus and the apostles spoke of 'the cross' as a principle of Christian experience as well as the chief symbol of God's love. Belonging to Jesus Christ, (he said), meant taking up the cross personally and living for him rather than for ourselves.

In *The Shadow of the Cross*, Walter Chantry restores this often neglected teaching to its central place. Writing with the stirring and probing sharp-edged style which is the hallmark of all his books, it expounds in brief compass the practical necessity of bearing the cross and the joy of living under its shadow. He then applies this to such areas as marriage, Christian liberty, the work of the ministry and prayer.

ISBN 0 85151 331 X
80pp., paperback

PRAISES FOR THE KING OF KINGS
Walter Chantry

Walter Chantry reminds us that in the seventeenth century Samuel Rutherford once exclaimed, 'Black sun, black moon, black stars, but, O bright, infinitely bright Lord Jesus.' His aim in *Praises for the King of Kings* is to produce a similar sense of admiration of Christ and praise for him in the present century. He therefore invites us to share in meditation on the person of Christ and his work through the study of three psalms which focus our gaze on different aspects of his grace, majesty and glory. Thus, in Psalm 2, we are introduced to a philosophy of life; in Psalm 110, we are given a vision of the coronation of Christ; in Psalm 45 we catch a glimpse of Christ in the glory of his return.

Praises for the King of Kings is a faithful exposition of these passages of Scripture, and illustrates what it means for us to fix our minds on Christ and have our hearts filled with his love. But it also throbs with praise for the King of Kings and leads to the kind of worship and admiration of the Messiah which David, Samuel Rutherford and countless others have experienced.

ISBN 0 85151 587 8
120pp., paperback.

A HEART FOR GOD
Sinclair B. Ferguson

A Heart for God is written out of the conviction that the world's greatest need – and the contemporary church's greatest lack – is the knowledge of God. In a popular, readable style it draws us to an awareness of the character of God and the nature of his relationship to his people.

In these pages, Sinclair B. Ferguson guides us, step-by-step, to see the greatness of God in his majesty and creating power; to sense the tenderness of his care and the marvel of his love. *A Heart for God* is 'Practical, pastoral and profound' (J. I. Packer). It unfolds the grace of God with a simple clarity which should lead each reader to pray (with John Calvin, the reformer): 'I offe my heart to you, Lord, eagerly and earnestly.'

Dr Sinclair B. Ferguson is Professor of Systematic Theology at Westminster Theological Seminary, Philadelphia, U.S.A., and is the author of a number of books also published by the Trust.

ISBN 0 85151 502 9
144pp., paperback

SOME FAVOURITE BOOKS
John Macleod

Some Favourite Books contains twenty-two miniature essays on some of the finest devotional and biographical literature of the Christian church.

Dr John Macleod invites us to join him as he selects great books from his book-case and introduces us to a great life or to some rich spiritual theme. Here are splendid introductions to such classics as Guthrie's *The Christian's Great Interest*, Rutherford's *Letters* and Ryle's *Christian Leaders* (all recently republished by the Trust). Here too we meet famous Christian leaders – John Knox, Charles Simeon and the Haldane brothers – but also lesser known heroes of the faith like John Blackader and Campbell of Kiltearn. Fascinating in its own right, *Some Favourite Books* also serves as an ideal introduction to great Christian literature. It is ideal for occasional reading and also as a tool to encourage others to read.

Dr John Macleod was Principal of the Free Church College, Edinburgh, and author of the classic work *Scottish Theology*.

ISBN 0 85151 538 X
128pp., paperback

Write for free 24pp. illustrated Catalogue to:
THE BANNER OF TRUTH TRUST
3 Murrayfield Road, Edinbrgh EH12 6EL
P.O. Box 621, Carlisle, Pennsylvania, 17013, U.S.A.